Dedication

To my father, who always believed in me

To my mother, who shared her love of baking with me

To my husband, who always encourages and supports me

To my children, Nerina, Joseph, Madeline, and Rebecca,
who continue to inspire me

MARY DISOMMA™
MARYDISOMMA.COM

My Life in Pies

SWEET AND SAVORY RECIPES INSPIRED BY FAMILY & FRIENDS

PHOTOGRAPHY BY PAUL STRABBING

FOOD & PROP STYLING BY JOHANNA BRANNAN LOWE

Mary DiSomma is as passionate about helping children as
she is about baking and is donating all proceeds from the sale
of this book to two Chicago-area children's charities.

Hephzibah Children's Association
and
The Oak Park River Forest Infant Welfare Society

Based in Mary's hometown of Oak Park, Illinois, these two
organizations have served the area for more than a century.
Hephzibah provides a safe place for vulnerable children and families
in need. The Infant Welfare Society takes a holistic approach to
pediatric primary care services, bringing greater health equity
and social justice to publicly insured and uninsured children.

For more information or to make a donation, please visit:
hephzibahhome.org
childrensclinicwis.org

Editor: **Mary DiSomma**
Recipe Editor: **Terri Milligan**
Writers: **Bill Strong, Anne-Marie St. Germaine**
Photography: **Paul Strabbing**
Food & Prop Styling: **Johanna Brannan Lowe**
Food Styling Assistants: **Jane Katte, Hawley Shoffner**
Art Direction & Design: **Deirdre Boland**
Graphic Design: **Brett Hawthorne**

Manufactured in China.
Mary DiSomma and the "M" Design are trademarks of Mary's Delishes, LLC.
ISBN: 979-8-218-97073-4

MARY DISOMMA™
marydisomma.com
Mary's Delishes, LLC
Oak Park, Illinois 60302 USA

"The joy of making
pie comes in combining
humble ingredients to create
a masterpiece to be shared and
savored by family and friends. When
I have a pie in the oven, it means
people will soon be gathering to
celebrate the harvest, achievements
large and small, holidays and
tradition—and life itself."

M

Table of Contents

The large wooden board, firmly grasped and skillfully wielded, is carefully set out on the kitchen counter, lightly floured as always.

Rolling pin in hand, the baker carefully and rhythmically rolls out the dough, a quarter-turn to the left or right every two rolls. Baking is all about precision, and sure enough, a near-perfect circle emerges from the small disc of dough–just as the shape of the festive day emerges from memory.

I loved working in the kitchen with my mom. When I was ready to progress from watching to taking the rolling pin in my own hands, she was patient in teaching me the techniques of making the perfect pie. I am grateful for these memories.

Given my mother's skills, our family became accustomed to homemade desserts. I don't ever recall her serving a store-bought pie. I'm sure it was the same with my grandmother.

This is my earliest recollection of baking pies in my mother's kitchen.

Recipe cards were the bible. My mother's pies were so beautiful and tasty because she worked from recipes passed down through generations–literally tried and true. In the quest for precision in baking, repetition is a virtue.

My mother never veered off course with her pies. Easter always brought her sweet ricotta pie and her savory Easter calzone. Thanksgiving was always a well-stuffed apple, mincemeat, and pumpkin pie. Christmas was more about cookies, but she would break out and bake an apple pie just for good measure.

Pies signify love. Love for family, friends, and tradition.

Nothing beats sitting around the table with family and friends and enjoying a slice of homemade pie. This is where we hear family stories and share dreams for the future.

Stories and dreams came together when our kids went to summer camp in the Boundary Waters Wilderness Area in Northern Minnesota. My husband and I eagerly anticipated picking them up after a backpack or canoe adventure and taking them to our favorite restaurant in Ely, Minnesota–Chocolate Moose. And yes, it was known for its pies.

What better way to hear about our children's adventures in the wilderness than sitting around the table together, enjoying a delicious piece of pie!

Tips, Tools, and Techniques

When baking with my mother, we always made sure to
have our trusty tools ready along with all our ingredients.
This chapter provides you with tons of information
about what you need to bake the perfect pie. Some
tips were learned from my mother and some from my
grandmother, plus a few I've learned along the way!

Baking Tips

Read your recipe all the way through before you start baking. Yes, this seems like a no-brainer, but don't lie. You probably have started a recipe then gotten to step 5 and discovered you didn't have an essential ingredient. It only takes a few minutes to do and it could be the difference between a pie star and a pie fail.

Measure and line up all those ingredients before you begin your pie baking. Get the right pie pan out along with parchment paper, nonstick cooking spray, and even the garnishes. Are you whipping cream in the recipe? Make sure the cream is chilled and the bowl cold. Butter? If it's softened to room temperature, make sure you have it out at least 30 minutes before you start your recipe. If you are using chilled, cubed butter, cut the butter into cubes then store in the refrigerator until needed.

MEASURING MATTERS

Use the right measuring cup. Dry ingredients like flour and sugar should be measured in a traditional measuring cup that goes to the top of the cup. Use a large spoon to fill the measuring cup, then level off the top with a knife. A quick sweep of a knife or straight-edged spatula removes the excess flour. Liquid measuring cups should be used for cream, milk, and water.

Sticky ingredients, like honey and molasses, can be difficult to measure. Here's my little trick. Before measuring, spray your measuring cup with nonstick cooking spray. Your sticky ingredients will slide right out.

INGREDIENT TEMPERATURE IS KEY

Ingredients work differently depending on their temperature. Eggs, especially egg whites, work best when room temperature. You will get much more volume than if your eggs are cold right out of the fridge.

Cream, on the other hand, should be cold. In fact, I even put my mixing bowl and wire whip attachment into the fridge to make sure everything involved in whipping that cream is well chilled. When it comes to preparing the perfect pie crust, the temperature of the fat is essential. The colder the better! Cutting or grating cold butter into small pieces will help it incorporate into the flour faster and more evenly.

DON'T GO OUT OF ORDER

Like any science, the science of baking requires that ingredients be added at certain times to create the best outcome. Follow the recipe as written. For example, eggs should be added one at a time. Eggs added all at once won't emulsify or blend together properly with the other ingredients. Additions like chocolate chips and nuts are often folded in by hand at the end of the recipe so the pie filling doesn't get overworked.

REMEMBER THE SALT!

When I first started baking, I didn't understand the value of adding salt when it was called for in a recipe. I've learned. Don't skip the salt! That little bit of salt will bring out the flavor of the other ingredients in the recipe.

CHECK YOUR OVEN TEMPERATURE

Make sure your oven is calibrated properly. Even if you have a fancy oven, I still recommend using an oven thermometer to make sure your oven temperature is correct.

CHILL OUT!

Chill in the fridge is my motto. Traditional butter or shortening-based pastry dough recipes should be refrigerated at least 30 minutes before being rolled out. Chilling the dough makes it much easier to roll out and transfer to your pie pan. If you have extra dough, no problem. Just wrap your dough disk with plastic wrap and label it with the date and the type of dough. The day before you are planning to make your pie, just pop it in the fridge and it will be ready to go. Chilling a pastry-lined crimped pie pan in the fridge also prevents the pastry from sliding down the pan side during baking.

FREEZING UNBAKED PIES

Face it; you don't always have the time to make and bake a pie. Having some frozen unbaked pies tucked away in the freezer can be a lifesaver when unexpected (or even expected) guests arrive at your doorstep. I especially like to freeze pies for the holidays so I can pull them out at a moment's notice.

Double-crust fruit pies are the easiest to freeze along with pies that have a streusel or crumb topping. When preparing pies that are going to be frozen, make sure that any filling that is added to the pastry-lined pie pan is completely cool. A warm filling poured on top of that raw dough will make it soggy and you'll never get the bottom crust to bake properly.

Forget about that egg wash. Pies that are going to be frozen should not be brushed with an egg wash glaze or sprinkled with sugar until you are ready to put them in the oven.

When your pies are filled and ready to go into the freezer, place them on a freezer rack, if you have a stand up freezer, or on a baking sheet. You need the pies to freeze on a level surface. Once frozen, remove the pies and wrap them in plastic wrap followed by aluminum foil. And make sure to label and mark the pie with the date and pie type. Although frozen pies are best used within 2 months, you can safely go to 4 or 5 months if they are properly wrapped.

Baking a frozen pie isn't that much different than baking a regular pie except you need about 15 percent more time in the oven. When ready to bake, preheat your oven to 425 degrees. While the oven is preheating, let the frozen pie sit at room temperature. It is best if the dough is slightly tacky before it hits the oven and about 15 minutes out of the freezer should do the trick. Remember to brush the top of the pie (if it is a double crust) with egg wash and sprinkle with sugar if desired. Wrap some aluminum foil around the edge of the pie so the crust doesn't brown too quickly.

Lower the temperature to 400 degrees. Place the pie on a baking sheet and put it on a rack that is just slightly lower than the middle of the oven. This will help the bottom crust fully cook. Bake the pie for 50 to 60 minutes. About 15 minutes before the pie is done, remove the foil so the crust edge finishes browning. The pie is ready when the crust is golden brown and the internal temperature of the pie is 200 degrees. Use an instant-read thermometer to check this. Remove the pie from the oven and let it cool on a wire rack.

AND ONE FINAL NOTE. TURN OFF THE PHONE!

Distractions are a baker's worst nightmare. Baking demands accuracy and care. No multi-tasking when measuring ingredients. Let the cell phone ring or better yet, put it on airplane mode or mute. You can always call someone back. But an overcooked pie is gone forever.

Ingredient Basics

Although each recipe varies, there are some essential basic ingredients you should have in your refrigerator and pantry.

FLOUR

Flour is made up of protein and starch. Bakers have to understand what makes up flour in order to select the right one. Ultimately, it is the protein content that determines how a flour reacts in a recipe.

Higher protein flours, like bread flour, are used when you are looking for flour that will hold up to yeast and baking agents. The protein level of bread flour is between 12 and 13 percent.

On the other end of the spectrum you will find pastry flour, with an 8 to 9 percent protein level, and cake flour clocking in at a 5 to 8 percent level. These lower protein flours are great for very tender baked goods like cakes, biscuits, and certain types of cookies.

All-purpose flour is recommended for most pie pastry recipes. Its protein content is about 8 to 10 percent, giving it enough stability to form a nice crust but still give you that tenderness you are looking for.

For those who are looking for a gluten-free pastry recipe, I have included my favorite. Because there is no gluten in the flour, the pastry tends to be a bit tricky to work with. It can break when rolled-out so don't be shy to give it a little pinch to fix any cracks that may occur when you place the raw rolled-out dough into your pie pan. Look for gluten-free flour that is marketed as a 1-to-1 flour, meaning 1 cup of gluten-free flour equals 1 cup of all-purpose flour.

FAT

Pie pastry always needs some sort of fat. It may be shortening, it may be butter, and it may be a little of both. It all depends on the recipe and, quite frankly, what you like. My favorite pie dough recipe falls in the combo area: half unsalted butter and half shortening. This combination creates a nice flaky crust because of the shortening and a pack of flavor from the butter.

Make sure that your butter is unsalted and cold before you start adding it to your flour. You can dice the chilled butter into cubes and place them in batches through a feed tube in your food processor or use a pastry blender to meld them by hand into your bowl of flour. Here's one of my favorite tips: to get really nice small shreds of butter (they'll incorporate easier into your flour), freeze your butter sticks and use a grater to shred the butter into thin shards.

If you are making a vegan or vegetarian version of my gluten-free crust, reach for a vegan butter alternative. The result will differ from using a butter or shortening base, but with a little tender loving care, you can create the perfect vegan crust.

EGGS

Size matters when it comes to eggs. Make sure you have the right size on hand before you start baking. All the recipes in this book call for large eggs.

WATER

The addition of water to your flour and fat mixture is the "glue" that binds your pastry crust together. Water, like butter, should be added cold. I usually place my cold water in a glass measuring cup with a spout along with a few ice cubes. This keeps that water super cold. Just make sure the ice cubes don't get into your flour mixture!

Another tip is to add that water slowly. Test the dough by placing a piece between your fingers. If it comes together, the dough is ready. If it is still crumbly, drizzle in a little more water. And don't fret if you add too much water. Just sprinkle in a little more flour. Pie dough is pretty forgiving.

HEAVY CREAM

I love topping or serving pie with mounds of whipped cream. Here are my 3 simple rules when working with whipped cream.

1. Buy the right cream (it's all about the fat content!) Whipping cream must be at least 30 percent fat. But heavy cream? Heavy cream must come in no less than 36 percent fat. That doesn't sound like a lot but those 6 percentage points of fat make a huge difference in the amount of volume you will get out of that cream.

2. Use only chilled heavy cream and a chilled bowl. The colder the cream, the better the result. Using a chilled bowl keeps the cream colder as well.

3. Add additions like sugar, after the cream starts holding a soft peak. Adding the sugar too early weighs down the cream and you won't get those lovely whipped cream peaks.

Pan Selection

There is more to a pie than the perfect crust recipe. The right pie pan matters. What makes for a great pan? Often it depends on the recipe. The material the baking dish is made of affects the final result. Metal, glass, and ceramic all conduct heat differently and therefore affect the pie's final outcome.

METAL PIE PANS

The most commonly used pie pan is 9-inches round and made of metal or aluminum. This pan wins the prize for producing crisp, golden crusts. These pans aren't fussy and are very economical. The metal ensures a fast, even heat which is perfect for pie baking–especially if you are blind baking (baking the crust without a filling).

Look for the lighter colored metal pans as darker ones have a higher heat absorption which can be overkill for pies. If you are making a pie that is going to be frozen, a metal pie pan is your best pick as it can be exposed to quick temperature changes.

GLASS PIE PANS

Tempered glass pie pans are safe to use in the oven, microwave, fridge, and freezer. These pans are made of either tempered or borosilicate glass. The latter is sturdier and less likely to break. Like metal pie pans, they are inexpensive, easy to find, and predictable. Glass heats at a slow and steady even pace, which promotes consistent baking and browning. Pastry baked in a glass pie pan does have a tendency to "slip" from shrinkage during the baking process so make sure your pastry-lined pie pan sits in the refrigerator to chill before placing it in the oven. I avoid using a glass pie pan if the pie is going to be frozen. Though they might not shatter, they still are made of glass and can break or crack.

Look for pans with oversized handles. You will be glad you did when it's time to pull your pie out of the oven. OXO™ makes a glass pie plate with a lid and is a great choice if you are traveling with your pie.

CERAMIC PIE PANS

These are by far the prettiest of the bunch. They are also the most expensive. All in all, these are my personal favorites. They provide the best of both worlds–they conduct slow, even heat and they are just plain pretty.

Many ceramic pans come with a thick rim. I find this makes fluting easier. These pie pans are often larger and deeper than the standard metal and glass pan versions. Keep this in mind when measuring out your fillings. Ceramic heats up more slowly than glass or metal so again, be prepared to adjust baking times as needed. Since ceramic pie pans are artisan-made, make sure to check the instructions that come with your pan to see how hot of an oven it can withstand and if it is freezer safe.

Stoneware is considered one of the most durable ceramics. Le Creuset™ happens to be one of my favorite brands. It's nonstick and so sturdy it resists cracking. And even though it heats up slower than metal or glass, I get a perfectly even crust every time.

TART PANS

Tart pans with removable bottoms are essential must-haves for any baker. This makes removing the delicate tarts from the pan easier. Many are nonstick which is also a great feature. I like to have a variety of sizes, from the traditional 9-inch round to square and oblong.

MINIATURE TART PANS

These classic French pans create the perfect single-serving tart. Who wouldn't love to have their very own miniature French tart for dessert?

HAND-HELD PIE MOLDS

I have several recipes in this book for hand pies. These wonderful little treats are basically a pie that is self-contained and fits in your hand. How wonderful is that? Though you can make them by cutting dough out into circles, triangles, or rectangles and folding it over the filling, you can also buy pre-made molds that form a perfect crescent-shaped pie. If you love hand pies as much as I do, I would recommend getting a mini-hand pie mold.

Essential Baking Tools

You can go crazy buying the next best gadget to make a perfect pie. But when it comes down to it, there are a few essential pieces of equipment that are must-haves in my kitchen.

DIGITAL KITCHEN SCALES

A kitchen scale is a bare essential. Weighing out nuts, chopped chocolate, and cheese is a breeze if you have a good kitchen scale. I prefer a digital scale so there is no question about the ingredient's weight.

FOOD PROCESSORS

A stand mixer gets all the glory in the kitchen. The food processor is the unsung hero. This machine is suited to an entirely different range of kitchen chores, from grinding nuts to making my favorite pie dough. Brands that I am fond of are Magimix™, Cuisinart™, and the Breville Sous Chef™. I also like to have a mini-food processor in the kitchen for quick, smaller jobs like chopping nuts and chocolate.

KITCHEN SCISSORS

The perfect tool to remove excess pie dough when assembling your pie.

Measuring Tools

MEASURING CUPS

There are separate measuring cups for wet and dry ingredients. Liquid and dry measuring cups do hold the same volume, the difference is that each is specially designed to do a better job of measuring its respective ingredients. Dry ingredient measures are designed to be filled to the brim and then leveled off with a knife. Wet ingredient measures are designed with markings that do not go all the way to the top to avoid spilling. Proper measurements are crucial in baking.

DRY MEASURING CUPS

Dry measuring cups come in various set sizes. The largest I have found is the 7-piece set which includes a 1, ¾, ⅔, ½, ⅓, ¼, and ⅛ cup measurements. When purchasing a set, make sure to look for cups with flat bottoms to prevent tipping when measuring.

LIQUID MEASURING CUPS

The Pyrex glass measuring cups are my personal favorite. They are dishwasher and microwave safe. Made of non-porous tempered glass, these sturdy cups won't absorb stains or odors. They are easy to clean, durable, high quality, and have easy-to-read measurements. They are great for mixing and pouring. These cups conveniently come in a 3-piece set which includes a 4, 2, and 1 cup measurement.

MEASURING SPOONS

Invest in a sturdy stainless steel set of measuring spoons. They come in various size sets, from 4 to 7 spoons. I like having the larger set that includes ⅛, ¼, ½, ¾, 1 teaspoon, ½ tablespoon, and 1 tablespoon measurements.

Mixers

STAND MIXER

This mighty machine is a game changer. Stand mixers don't require the babysitting or upper body strength needed with other equipment. This stationary motor-powered work of wonder usually comes with 3 attachments: a paddle, wire whisk, and dough hook. These attachments allow you to do everything from whipping cream to kneading dough. You can also get additional attachments for juicing and grinding. I recommend the bowl-lift variety that has an oversized bowl. The tilt-head version is slightly smaller and is a great budget-friendly choice.

HAND MIXER

Although the stand mixer is the baking work horse, sometimes you still need a handheld mixer. Look for one that has 5 speeds. This mixer is handy for whipping small amounts of egg whites or whipped cream.

MIXING BOWLS

A complete set of glass or metal mixing bowls will prove to be invaluable. Make sure when purchasing glass bowls that they are tempered, meaning they can take the heat if placed in a microwave.

PASTRY BAGS AND TIPS

Pastry bags are made from various materials and are available in lengths ranging from 7 to 24 inches. You can find plastic-lined cloth bags, nylon bags, and canvas bags. The disposable plastic bags make for the easiest clean-up since you simply toss them when you're done. If you would rather have one all-purpose bag, choose a 14- to 16-inch plastic-lined cloth bag. For decorating pies with whipped cream or meringue, I use a large star tip but it's always nice to have a few smaller tips to decorate individual tarts. Hand wash bags and tips with warm soapy water and then stand them, tip side up, to air-dry.

PASTRY BRUSH

This tool has countless uses. For pies, this brush is used to apply egg washes and remove excess flour from your dough. It is also great for buttering pans. They are usually made with boar bristles which are soft and flexible for easy thorough brushing. Pastry brushes are also available made out of silicone—a good bet if you are looking for a brush that can take a high heat of 500 degrees.

PASTRY BOARDS

A high-quality, durable pastry board that can withstand daily use is a baking tool essential. Your countertop will thank you. They are made of plastic, wood, or marble. Because of its cooling properties, marble boards are a great choice when working with pastry doughs that have a high butter content like puff pastry. The marble surface remains cooler than room temperature. This keeps the butter from getting too warm while rolling out your dough.

PASTRY MAT WITH MEASUREMENTS

This mat is perfect for rolling out pastry dough. A silicone pastry mat is slip-proof with handy measurements to guide you as you roll out your dough into a perfect circle. No ruler needed to make sure your pie dough is rolled out to the correct measurement.

PARCHMENT PAPER

Having a supply of parchment paper is a must for any pie baker. Lining a tart pan with parchment paper makes removal of the finished tart a snap. After removing the pan side, the parchment paper allows you to simply push the tart onto a serving platter, leaving the metal bottom behind.

Rolling Pins

When it comes to rolling pins, quality matters. If you're like me, you may have been lucky enough to have inherited your mother's or grandmother's rolling pin. A good quality rolling pin can be kept forever, handed down from generation to generation to love and enjoy.

THE AMERICAN OR BAKERS ROLLING PIN

This classic rolling pin, with its cylindrical roller and rod running through the center, is fitted with ball bearings with two easy-to-hold handles. Generally made from wood, this pin is a great "first rolling pin" and is used most often by recreational bakers. The heavier the pin, the less arm strength needed. Water is not a friend to any rolling pin. The best way to clean a rolling pin is to brush off excess dough bits then wipe with a clean dry towel. If a wooden pin becomes dry, bring it back to life with a rub of mineral oil.

MARBLE ROLLING PIN

In addition to being beautiful to look at, marble rolling pins shine when working with heat-sensitive dough. Bring out the marble rolling pin when working with puff pastry and butter-heavy doughs. These durable and easy-to-clean pins work best when dusted with a bit of flour prior to starting the rolling process.

FRENCH ROLLING PIN

A French pin is basically a long stick with tapered ends. This is a great pin for bakers who want to graduate from the American pin to a French-style pin. Working with a French rolling pin requires a bit of practice. Use your hands to guide the pin, adding a bit of muscle to form a smooth dough. Rotate the dough between rolls to create a circular round of pastry.

ROLLING DOWELS

Rolling dowels are a cousin to the French rolling pin. Like a French pin, rolling dowels do not have handles. But instead of having a tapered look, rolling dowels have a long smooth cylinder shape.

ADJUSTABLE ROLLING PIN AND ROLLING PIN RINGS

This pin takes the guesswork out of dough thickness. The rolling pin comes with adjustable rings that come in 4 different sizes. I favor one made by Joseph Joseph®. The pin does the work for you, creating an accurate and uniform dough thickness. You can also purchase rolling pin rings that work on most rolling pins. These rings make sure your dough is rolled out to the perfect thickness every time.

BAKING SHEETS

If you are going to have just one baking sheet in your kitchen, make it a heavy commercial-grade baker's sheet. These baking gems are made of 10- to 18-gauge aluminum, the material of choice for manufacturers due to its affordable price, durability, high heat conductivity, and efficiency. Though you don't need a baking sheet to make a pie, I often place my pies on one during the baking process to catch any filling that may boil over. It also makes removing the baked pie from the oven easier.

SIFTER

Sifters remove lumps and aerate flour, confectioners' sugar, cocoa powder, or other fine, dry ingredients. I prefer a sturdy stainless steel sifter with a hand crank.

SILICONE SPATULA

You will definitely need one of these handy to mix delicate fillings. They are durable and can survive high temperatures up to 500 degrees Fahrenheit.

OVEN THERMOMETERS

Ovens tend to have a mind of their own when it comes to temperature accuracy. You can easily become its master by purchasing a dial display thermometer.

CANDY THERMOMETER

Don't confuse a candy thermometer with a meat thermometer. A candy thermometer is designed just for working with hot syrups and sugars. I suggest purchasing a digital version which is easier to read. And when it comes to heating sugar syrup for something like my meringue recipe, a few degrees too high or low makes all the difference in your finished product.

PIE WEIGHTS

Many of the recipes in this book call for blind baking your pastry shell. Simply put, blind baking is baking the raw pie shell without a filling. Some sort of pie weight is essential for this process. Ceramic pie weights are washable and reusable and available at most cooking supply stores and online. If you don't have ceramic pie weights, there are many items in your pantry that you can use. Dried beans, like kidney and pinto, work great as well as raw rice. I like to cool them after use and put them in a plastic food bag or plastic container. Store them in the pantry until they are needed for your next pie. Another good pie weight hack is to use granulated sugar. Just remember to mark that it has been used as pie weights.

WIRE RACK

When your hot pie comes out of the oven, it can be placed on a wire rack to cool.

Additional Tools

Once you have your pie baking essentials, you can expand into some special gadgets that can make your pie baking easier.

BENCH SCRAPER

This tool helps pick up and move your dough. I like to have one that is metal and one that is plastic. The plastic version, which is more flexible, is great to scrape out whipped cream and meringue from a mixing bowl. The metal version helps lift pie pastry and transfer it to a pie pan.

CHERRY PITTER

You can purchase either multi or single cherry pitters. This is a time saving tool and makes pitting cherries a breeze.

COOKIE CUTTERS

Have a variety of smaller shaped cookie cutters in your pie-making arsenal so you can embellish the top of your pies with pastry-shaped leaves, stars, and small flowers. I like to use pop-out cutters. These small cutters have a spring on them that when pressed, pops the cut pastry right out. A round 4-inch cutter comes in handy when making hand pies and empanadas. You can also find a special tool to place the filled 4-inch pastry round on, with the tool flipping one side of the pastry and sealing it.

DOUGH BLENDER

This tool helps incorporate butter and shortening into dry ingredients without overworking or over-warming the dough. It has 5 slender blades that help you achieve optimal blending.

MICROPLANE

A microplane zester can be used for grating everything from citrus zest to fresh ginger and even chocolate. I avoid putting my microplane in the dishwasher as it can dull the sharp blades. It comes with a handy cover to go over the blade. Use it! It will keep that blade nice and sharp.

PASTRY WHEEL

Pastry wheels are available with a straight or fluted edge. This tool makes creating strips of dough for a lattice-top pie a breeze.

PIE CARRIERS

Make for easy pie transport.

PIE TOP CUTTER

This tool makes it simple to create a decorative top for your homemade pie. It quickly cuts a perfect lattice from a single piece of dough.

PIE SHIELD

A silicone or metal adjustable pie crust shield helps prevent overbrowning of your pie crust edge. It is designed to be placed along the exposed edge of the crust during baking. You can use aluminum foil to do the job but this shield is more effective and easier to use. It is reusable too. Put the shield on your pie before you put it in the oven, then remove it toward the end of the bake time to achieve your desired level of browning.

RULER OR SOFT MEASURING TAPE

This comes in handy when you need to measure your rolled-out dough to ensure it is big enough to accommodate your pie pan.

WOOD PIE BOXES

These decorative boxes make it easy to transport pies and are great for gift giving.

All About Crusts

I learned how to make pie dough as a little girl in my mother's kitchen. We didn't have a food processor to make the blending of the ingredients easier. Back then it was with a pastry blender, the two-knife method, or just your good-old hands.

Although you can certainly use those tried and true methods to incorporate the cold butter or shortening into your flour mixture, I rely heavily on my food processor to do the work. Plus I can make several batches of dough and freeze them for later use.

My mom's pie crusts always came out perfect even though she didn't have all the fancy gadgets available today. I think it's because of all the love she put into her baking.

What Makes a Perfect Pie Dough?

A pie dough recipe needs to have the perfect ratio of flour to fat to some sort of liquid to bind it all together. And don't forget the salt. A little salt brings out the flavor of the pastry.

For flour, use an all-purpose blend unless you are making my gluten-free crust. Then make sure to use a gluten-free flour that is listed as 1 to 1, meaning 1 cup of gluten-free flour equals 1 cup of all-purpose flour.

For the fat portion, I vary in what I use. You can go all in on either shortening or unsalted butter, or do what I do. Use both! The pie dough recipe I use the most in this book is my Favorite Pie Dough recipe that blends the benefits of shortening and butter together.

When I want a real buttery crust or am making a pie that has a European influence, I lean towards using a traditional pâte brisée pastry. This classic pie dough is made with only butter and tends to be super flavorful.

For a sweeter crust, use a pâte sucrée pastry. It's basically a buttery pie dough with a little sugar in it. This dough is perfect for delicate fruit tarts, especially in miniature form.

Cold is the Word

When you make pie dough, think cold. Cold butter cubes, cold water added to the mixture, and most importantly, cold dough when you are literally ready to roll.

Butter should be in the form of chilled cubes when being added through the food processor feed tube. If you are making the dough in a mixing bowl and using a pastry blender, try this trick. Freeze the butter in stick form then use a box grater. Grate the frozen butter into small thread-like pieces and place in your mixing bowl with your flour and salt. The butter will uniformly meld with the flour with some good twists of the pastry blender.

Rolling Your Dough

Most pie pans are 9-inches round. That means you should roll your dough into an 11-inch circle so you have plenty of overhang to create the perfect edge.

Take your chilled dough disk out of the refrigerator about 10 minutes before you are ready to roll. Lightly dust your work surface and place the disk in the center. Then roll, turning the dough at a 45-degree angle every few rolls until you get an 11-inch circle. Fold the dough into quarters then transfer it to your prepared pie pan.

For more tender doughs, like a pâte sucrée or gluten-free pastry, roll the dough between two pieces of lightly floured (all-purpose or gluten-free) parchment paper. Use the bottom piece of parchment paper to transfer the dough into your prepared pie pan.

Creating Your Pie Pastry Edge

Now the fun starts! The pastry overhang can be transformed into a variety of fantastic edges. There's the traditional fluted edge or the crimped edge with a fork indentation. But there's also ways to make your pies a work of art by adding a braided edge, a leaf, or a flower edge using small cookie cutters.

Crimped Edge with a Fork

Crimped Edge

Cut-out Edge

Braided Edge

Making a Lattice Crust

Begin by rolling out a piece of dough into a 12-inch circle. Now, use a knife or pastry wheel to cut out eleven ¼-inch strips of dough.

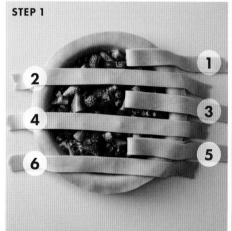

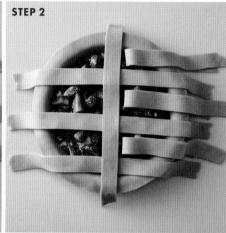

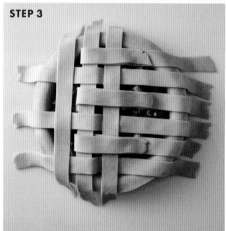

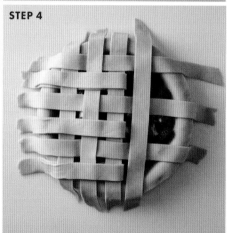

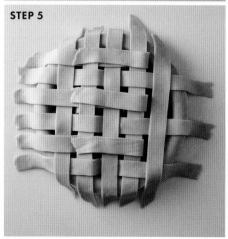

Step 1 Place 6 of the pieces on top of the pie horizontally, about ⅛-inch apart. Use the longer strips in the center of the pie and the shorter strips on the side.

Now, fold strips 1, 3, and 5 halfway back to the right.

Step 2 Place one piece of dough in the center of the pie. Unfold strips 1, 3, and 5 so they go over the strip you just placed in the center of the pie.

Step 3 Fold strips 2, 4, and 6 to the right over the strip of pastry. Place a piece of pastry to the left of the folded pastry strip. Unfold strips 2, 4, and 6.

Fold strips 1, 3, and 5 to the right. Place the shortest piece of pastry to the left and unfold strips 1, 3, and 5.

Step 4 and 5 Continue this weaving method on the other side of the pie with the 2 remaining strips of pastry.

Step 6 Trim the dough side and gently press to adhere lattice strips to the pie edge. Crimp the edge of the pie dough if desired.

Blind Baking

Many recipes call for a pie crust to be "blind baked." Simply put, blind baking just means baking the crust without the filling in it.

Sometimes the pie crust will be fully blind baked and sometimes it will be partially blind baked, meaning that the bottom crust is still a bit undercooked. A partially blind baked crust is often used if there is a baked filling, but it requires less than 20 minutes to bake.

To blind bake a crust, preheat your oven to 350 degrees. Chill your pastry-lined pie pan in the refrigerator or freezer for 30 minutes. Raw pastry that is cold will be less likely to shrink when it hits the heat of the oven.

Remove the pan from the refrigerator or freezer. Line the chilled pie crust with parchment paper. Evenly place ceramic pie weights, raw dried beans like pinto or kidney or raw rice on the parchment paper. If you don't have any of these items, you can even use sugar! Just make sure if you use dried beans or rice, you don't use them for any other purpose. Just let them cool at room temperature and place them in a ziplock bag to be used in the future. You can use them over and over!

For a fully blind baked pie shell, bake until the edges of the crust start to brown, about 15 to 16 minutes. Remove from the oven and carefully lift the parchment paper (with the weights) out of the pie pan. Using a fork, make 6 light pricks in the bottom of the crust, being careful not to go all the way through. Return pie crust to the oven and bake for 8 to 12 minutes or until the bottom of the crust is light brown. Remove from the oven and let cool on a rack for 15 minutes before filling the pie or tart.

For a partially baked pie shell, bake initially for 12 minutes, remove the parchment and weights and prick the bottom of the crust with a fork, then bake again for 3 minutes. Remove from the oven and let cool on a rack for 15 minutes before filling the pie or tart.

This is one of my favorite "go-to" pie crusts. It includes shortening as well as butter which I think makes the crust extra tender and flavorful. It's great for both a sweet or savory pie.

Mary's Favorite Pie Dough

Makes enough for 2 pie crusts or 1 double-crust pie

3 cups all-purpose flour

1 teaspoon kosher salt

1 tablespoon granulated sugar

1 cup (8 ounces) unsalted cold butter, very cold, cut into small pieces

⅓ cup very cold vegetable shortening

6 to 8 tablespoons (about ½ cup) ice water

1. Place the flour, salt, and sugar in the bowl of a food processor fitted with a steel blade. Pulse a few times to combine. With the processor on, add the cold butter through the feed tube, a few pieces at a time. Once the butter is incorporated, add the shortening a little at a time. Pulse 8 to 10 times until the butter and shortening form pea size pieces.

2. With the machine running, add enough ice water through the feed tube until the dough begins to form a ball. Be careful not to get any actual ice into the mixture. If the dough gets too wet, simply pulse in a little more flour. Place the dough on a lightly floured work surface and form into a ball.

3. Divide the ball in half and slightly flatten each ball with the palm of your hand. This will make rolling out the dough easier once it is chilled. Wrap the 2 dough pieces separately in plastic wrap and refrigerate for 30 minutes or overnight. Remove the dough from the refrigerator and roll out as needed for the pie you are preparing.

Tip: This dough is very versatile and can be used for both sweet and savory pies and tarts. I like to make a double or triple batch and freeze the individual dough disks for future use. Make sure to label the dough with the date. How nice to have pie dough ready to go! The frozen dough will last 2 months in the freezer. Thaw the dough overnight in the refrigerator, removing it 30 minutes before you're ready to roll!

Pâte brisée is a handy and versatile pastry dough that's useful for a variety of dishes (both sweet and savory), including pies, tarts and quiches. This French-based pastry is similar to my Mary's Favorite Pie Dough recipe, but differs in that it's made with all butter.

Pâte Brisée

Makes enough for 2 pie crusts or 1 double-crust pie

2¾ cups all-purpose flour, plus more as needed

1 teaspoon salt

1 cup (8 ounces) unsalted cold butter, cut into small pieces or frozen in stick form and shredded

¼ to ⅓ cup ice water

1. Place the flour and salt in the bowl of a food processor fitted with the steel blade. With the motor on, add the butter through the feed tube. Process 10 to 15 seconds. The dough should resemble a coarse meal.

2. With the machine running, add enough ice water through the feed tube until the dough begins to form a ball. Be careful not to get any ice into the mixture. If the dough gets too wet, simply pulse in a little more flour. Place the dough on a lightly floured work surface and form into a ball.

3. Divide the dough into 2 equal pieces. Form each piece into a ball, then flatten each with the palm of your hand. Wrap disks with plastic wrap and refrigerate at least 30 minutes before rolling out. The raw pastry dough can be frozen for up to 2 months. Thaw dough overnight in the refrigerator.

Pâte sucrée is a sweeter, more tender crust that's perfect for a dessert tart or miniature tarts. The addition of confectioners' sugar makes the dough a bit trickier to work with but don't fret! If you have any tears or cracks in the raw dough when you place it in your pie or tart pan, just use your fingers to press it back together.

Pâte Sucrée (Sweet Pastry Crust)

Makes enough for 2 pie crusts or 1 double-crust pie

3 cups all-purpose flour

⅔ cup confectioners' sugar

1 cup (8 ounces) cold unsalted butter, cut into small pieces

2 large egg yolks

2 to 4 tablespoons cold water, as needed

1. In the bowl of a food processor, combine the flour and confectioners' sugar. Pulse to combine. Add the cold butter into the flour mixture by placing the pieces slowly through the feed tube. Pulse as butter is being added.

2. Add the egg yolks, one at a time, along with enough of the cold water until the mixture is just moistened enough that when you place some dough in your hand and press it stays together.

3. Place the dough on a work surface and form into 2 balls. Using the palm of your hand, press each ball into a disk. Cover with plastic wrap and refrigerate for at least 2 hours. Wrapped in plastic wrap, the dough disk can be frozen for up to 2 months for future use. Thaw overnight in the refrigerator then roll out as directed in your recipe.

This chocolate cookie crust is the base of so many wonderful pies. It's the perfect match for a no-bake pie. I love to use mint creme Oreos when making my Grasshopper Pie. Who doesn't love a 2 ingredient recipe?!

Oreo™ Cookie Crust

Makes enough for one 9-inch pie

1 (15.25 ounce) package mint creme or regular Oreos

6 tablespoons (3 ounces) unsalted butter, melted

1. Break the cookies into pieces and place into a food processor. Process until the mixture turns into fine crumbs.

2. In a mixing bowl, combine the processed Oreos with the melted butter. Stir to combine. Transfer the mixture to the bottom and around the side of a 9-inch pie pan or springform pan with a removable bottom. Using your fingers, press the crumbs firmly into the bottom and side of the pan. Refrigerate or freeze the lined pan for 30 minutes before proceeding with your recipe.

I love graham crackers. If you love them as much as I do, you may want to make 1½ recipes of this easy crust so your pie is extra graham crackery. Whether the crust is baked or not depends on the recipe. And if you like chocolate, try using chocolate graham crackers for the recipe.

Mary's Favorite Graham Cracker Crust

Makes one 9-inch pie crust

2 cups crushed graham crackers or chocolate graham crackers (32 squares)

⅓ cup granulated sugar

8 tablespoons (4 ounces) unsalted butter, melted and slightly cooled

1. If the graham crackers are whole, place them in a food processor and pulse until ground to crumb consistency. In a mixing bowl, combine the crumbs and sugar. Add the melted butter and mix to blend. Spray a 9-inch pie pan or springform pan with nonstick cooking spray. Transfer the crumb mixture to the pan. Firmly press the crumb mixture on the bottom and side of the pan.

2. Refrigerate or freeze the crust for 30 minutes before baking and/or filling.

Here's my tip for this recipe: The crust mixture needs to be firmly pressed into the pan. I start by using my fingers, but then switch over to using a glass with a flat bottom. Press the bottom of the glass on top of the crust to really get the mixture firmly in place. Also remember to refrigerate or freeze the crust before baking it. That extra chill will firm up the butter and make the crust less lightly to sink when baking.

When preparing a gluten-free pie crust, make sure to use a flour that is listed as a 1-to-1 ratio. This means that 1 cup of gluten-free flour equals 1 cup of all-purpose flour.

The texture of this dough makes it a bit crumblier than a traditional pie dough. To make it easier to roll out, try dusting a piece of parchment paper with gluten-free flour. Place the chilled dough disk on top of the parchment paper and top with another piece of parchment paper. Roll out the dough (rolling on top of the second piece of parchment paper). Remove the top parchment paper and use the bottom piece of parchment paper to transfer the rolled-out dough to your prepared pie or tart pan.

If you want to make this tart dairy-free, vegan, or vegetarian, simply use vegan butter instead of unsalted butter.

Gluten-Free Pie Dough

Makes enough for one 9-inch pie or tart

2 cups 1-to-1 gluten-free flour

2 tablespoons sugar

½ teaspoon salt

½ cup vegan butter or unsalted butter, cold, cut into small pieces

4 to 5 tablespoons cold water

1. In the bowl of a food processor, combine the gluten-free flour, sugar, and salt. Pulse to combine.

2. Add the chilled vegan butter or unsalted butter, a few cubes at a time, through the feed tube, pulsing with each addition. Slowly add the water, 1 tablespoon at a time, through the feed tube, again pulsing after each addition until the dough comes together. You may not need all 5 tablespoons of water.

3. Remove the dough from the food processor and form it into a ball. Using the palm of your hand, press the dough into a disk. Wrap in plastic wrap and refrigerate for 30 minutes before rolling out.

Tip: Gluten-free pie crust can be challenging to work with. Luckily, it is very forgiving. If you happen to have some cracks or tears in the pastry after you transfer it to the pie or tart pan, just use your fingers to push the dough together or use scraps of the pastry to patch tears.

Heritage Pies

These recipes are especially near and dear to me—passed down in my family from generation to generation. Often they are simply handwritten on a note card with frayed edges from years of use, and love.

I've also included in this chapter recipes collected from travels throughout the world, shared with me by special friends and what I like to call my "adopted family." As a teenager, I spent time in Argentina, so in addition to family recipes, I am sharing recipes with an Argentinian flare.

My arroz con leche tarts, torta Pasqualina, and pasta frola tart were born from my love of Argentina and my memories of living there during high school. My take on knafeh came to life from recipes I learned from dear friends during travels to Turkey.

Each time I make one of these pies it reminds me of the people, place, and time associated with the recipe. These are truly the treasures in this book. I hope you adopt a few and share them with friends and family.

This savory Italian pie is a signature dish in our house at Easter. It's good enough to serve year-round, so I keep a few frozen, unbaked. I take the pie out of the freezer the night before baking. It's so popular in our house, I serve it on Christmas Eve. The dough for the Torta Rustica is a bit sturdier than most pie crusts—strong enough to hold all that delicious filling. Let the Torta Rustica rest for 30 minutes before cutting. It has to cool just a bit to firm up the filling. Be prepared to wow your guests with this one!

Torta Rustica

Makes one 9-inch torta in a springform pan

Prep Time: 1 hour
Baking Time: 50 minutes to 1 hour

Dough

4 cups all-purpose flour

1 teaspoon salt

1 cup (8 ounces) unsalted cold butter, cubed and set at room temperature for 15 minutes

2 large eggs plus 2 large egg yolks, beaten

⅓ cup whole milk

Filling

48 ounces frozen chopped spinach, thawed and squeezed dry with paper toweling

2 tablespoons extra-virgin olive oil

1 medium onion, diced

4 large eggs

1 cup finely grated Parmesan cheese

1 cup seasoned breadcrumbs

Salt and pepper to taste

Additional Filling Options

½ pound sliced fontina cheese

½ pound frozen tortellini, thawed

1 (4 ounce) jar pimentos, drained

8 ounces artichoke heart quarters, drained

1 cup sun-dried tomatoes, softened in warm water, drained and patted dry
or
1 cup oil-packed sun-dried tomatoes, drained (a little oil is fine)

Glaze

1 large egg

2 tablespoons heavy cream

1. In the bowl of a stand mixer fitted with the paddle attachment, combine the flour, salt, and a little of the cubed butter. Mix on low speed, adding the remaining butter cubes until small crumbs form.

2. In a separate bowl, whisk together the eggs, egg yolks, and milk. On medium speed, add the egg mixture to the flour mixture. Mix on low until a dough forms and begins to pull away from the side of the bowl. Remove dough from bowl and wrap in plastic wrap. Store in the refrigerator to rest. It is best to let dough rest in the refrigerator for at least 45 minutes before rolling it out.

3. Prepare the filling and torta: Thoroughly drain the frozen spinach and squeeze out extra moisture using paper toweling.

4. In a large sauté pan, heat the olive oil on medium heat. Add the onion and spinach. Sauté until onions are translucent but not browned.

5. In a large mixing bowl, combine the spinach, onion, eggs, Parmesan, and breadcrumbs. Season with salt and pepper to taste.

6. Prepare your springform pan: Line the bottom of a 9-inch springform pan with a round piece of parchment paper. Spray the side of the pan with nonstick cooking spray. Divide the chilled dough into 2 pieces. One piece will consist of ⅔ of the dough and the other with the remaining third. The larger piece of dough will line the bottom and side of the pan. Lightly flour a work surface and roll out the larger piece into a 14-inch circle. Fold the dough into fourths so you can easily pick it up and place it in the prepared pan. Gently unfold the dough and press it to adhere to the pan side. The dough should go all the way up the side of the pan. If you have any tears in the pastry, don't fret! Just use a little extra dough to mend any tears.

7. Now it's time to create your torta! Layer the ingredients using whatever additional fillings you select. I, of course, love them all. Here is the layering order I suggest: ½ of the spinach mix, ⅓ of the fontina cheese, tortellini, pimento, ⅓ of the fontina cheese, artichoke hearts, sun-dried tomatoes, remaining fontina cheese, and remaining spinach mixture. *(continued)*

Torta Rustica
Continued

8. Roll out the remaining dough and place on top of the torta, pinching the edges together with the bottom pastry. Roll out any remaining remnants of dough and cut into decorations for the top of the torta. Place decorations on a separate baking sheet lined with parchment. Refrigerate the torta and decorations overnight.

9. When ready to bake, preheat the oven to 375 degrees. Place torta on a parchment-lined baking sheet. Mix the remaining large egg with 2 tablespoons of cream. Brush egg glaze on top of the torta. Place the decorative cutouts on top and brush them with some of the glaze. Bake for approximately 50 minutes to 1 hour or until the torta is golden brown. Remove from the oven and let rest for 30 minutes. Carefully remove the springform ring. Serve warm or at room temperature.

Note: The unbaked torta can be frozen for up to a month. Remove from the freezer the night before you plan to bake it, and let it defrost in the refrigerator overnight. Remove from the fridge and bake for 1 hour 15 minutes to 1½ hours. If the top is beginning to brown too much, place a piece of foil on the top for the last ½ hour of baking.

When I lived with my foreign exchange family in Argentina, I always looked forward to their torta de papa. It was a simple dish but so delicious. To me, it was the ultimate comfort food. Their recipe was the inspiration for my Potato and Cheese Pie. I added a delicious crust along with fresh rosemary and pancetta. The crust is so divine, you can almost eat it without the filling!

Potato and Cheese Pie

Makes one 9-inch pie or a 1-quart oval casserole

Prep Time: 45 minutes
Baking Time: 1 hour

Savory Cheese Pastry Crust

2¼ cups all-purpose flour, plus additional for dusting work surface

½ cup finely grated Parmesan cheese
or
white cheddar cheese

½ teaspoon salt

¾ cup (6 ounces) cold unsalted butter, cut into small pieces

1 large egg yolk

¼ cup to ½ cup ice water

Filling

1½ pounds Yukon gold potatoes, peeled and thinly sliced

3 sprigs fresh rosemary

1 large egg

¾ cup heavy cream

¼ teaspoon salt

⅛ teaspoon white pepper

⅛ teaspoon ground nutmeg

3 ounces cooked pancetta or bacon, crumbled

1 cup grated Parmesan
or
cheddar cheese

Egg Wash

1 large egg yolk

1 tablespoon heavy cream

Optional Garnish

Fresh rosemary

Cooked pancetta or bacon, chopped or crumbled

1. In the bowl of a food processor, combine the flour, cheese, and salt. Pulse to combine. With the processor on, add the chilled butter cubes through the feed tube, a few at a time. Once incorporated, add the egg yolk followed by enough of the ice water to the mixture until the dough forms a firm, but not sticky, ball. If you accidentally add too much water, simply add a bit more flour. This is a forgiving dough!

2. Form the dough into a ball and flatten with the palm of your hand. Wrap loosely in plastic wrap and refrigerate while preparing the filling.

3. Preheat the oven to 350 degrees. Thinly slice the potatoes and place them in a large mixing bowl. I like to use a mandoline slicer for this. Believe me, it's a tool you will find many uses for in your kitchen. Place the sliced potatoes in a microwavable dish and add about ½-inch of water. Cover the dish with plastic wrap and microwave for 2 to 4 minutes. The potatoes should still be slightly firm but still be easily pierced with a paring knife. Drain the potatoes and reserve.

4. Remove the needles from the rosemary sprig and finely chop. In a small mixing bowl, combine the egg, cream, salt, white pepper, and nutmeg. Have the pancetta or bacon and cheese in small bowls as well. Once the pie dough is in the pan, you will want to have all the other ingredients ready to go!

5. Lightly flour your work surface. Roll the chilled dough out into an 11-inch circle. Place the dough into a 9-inch pie pan. Trim the dough as needed and crimp or flute the edge. If using an oval casserole dish, roll the dough into an oval shape.

6. Sprinkle ¼ cup of the cheese over the bottom of the tart. Add ⅓ of the potatoes in an even layer. Sprinkle with ¼ cup cheese, some of the fresh rosemary and ½ of the pancetta/bacon. Add another ⅓ layer of potatoes followed by ¼ cup cheese, the remaining rosemary and pancetta/bacon. Finish with the final layer of potatoes and the remaining ¼ cup cheese.

7. Place the pie on a baking sheet. Carefully pour the egg and cream mixture over the potato filling. In a small bowl, combine the egg yolk and cream. Brush the side of the pastry dough with the egg wash. Place the pie in the preheated oven and bake for 50 minutes to 1 hour or until lightly browned. Insert a toothpick into the center of the pie. It should go easily through the potatoes if they are done. Remove from the oven and let rest for 15 minutes before slicing. If desired, garnish with fresh rosemary and bacon or pancetta pieces.

This traditional pie is often served at Easter. I treasure the tattered recipe card written by my Mom with lots of love but minimal (zero!) directions. Her version does not include a crust, but I like the creamy filling to have a cozy resting place. My recipe remains full of love, but with directions! *Tip:* Don't worry about tears here and there when you place the rolled-out, soft dough in the pie pan. Just pinch together to fix the tears. I blind bake the crust so the bottom pastry won't get soggy after adding the filling.

Mom's Sweet Ricotta Pie

Makes one 9-inch pie

Prep Time: 1 hour
Baking Time: 1 hour and 45 minutes (includes blind baking crust and baking the pie)

Pie Pastry Dough

1½ cups all-purpose flour
¼ cup confectioners' sugar
¼ teaspoon baking powder
1 teaspoon lemon zest
¼ teaspoon salt
½ cup (4 ounces) unsalted butter, chilled and cut into ½-inch pieces
1 large egg

Filling

2 cups whole milk ricotta cheese
¾ cup sugar
4 large eggs, beaten
1 teaspoon anise extract
or
anise-flavored liqueur

1. In a food processor, combine the flour, confectioners' sugar, baking powder, lemon zest, and salt. Pulse to combine. With the food processor on, slowly add the chilled butter pieces through the feed tube. With the motor still running, add the egg and process for about 30 seconds until you have a cohesive ball of dough. Remove dough and form into a ball. Use the palm of your hand to form the ball into a disk. Wrap in plastic wrap and refrigerate for 30 minutes before rolling out.

2. Place the dough between 2 sheets of lightly floured parchment paper and roll out the dough into an 11-inch round. If it is a bit too sticky, just dust it lightly with a little flour. Remove the first sheet of parchment and use the other piece to transfer the dough to your pie pan. Don't worry if there are a few tears in the pastry. Just use your fingers to pinch the dough together to fix any tears. Using kitchen scissors, trim the edge of the dough, leaving ¾-inch of overhang. Crimp or flute the side of the dough and refrigerate or freeze for 30 minutes.

3. Preheat the oven to 350 degrees. Remove the pan from the refrigerator or freezer and blind bake the crust. Line the chilled pie crust with parchment paper. Fill with pie weights or dried beans. Make sure the weights are evenly distributed around the pan bottom. Bake until the edges of the crust are starting to brown, about 15 to 16 minutes. Remove from the oven and carefully lift the parchment paper (with the weights) out of the pie tin. Using a fork, make 6 light pricks in the bottom of the crust, being careful not to go all the way through. Return pie crust to the oven and bake for 8 minutes or until the bottom of the crust is light brown. Remove from the oven and let cool on a rack for 15 minutes before filling the tart. For more information on blind baking a crust, see page 29.

4. It's time to make the filling. Place a strainer over a bowl. Put the ricotta cheese in the strainer and let sit for 30 minutes to remove any excess liquid. Place the strained ricotta in a mixing bowl. Whisk in the sugar followed by the eggs and the anise flavoring. *(continued)*

Mom's Sweet Ricotta Pie

Continued

5. We are going to bake the pie in the oven using a water-bath method. This method will keep the filling from becoming too dry during the baking process. Preheat the oven to 350 degrees. Place 7 cups of water in a pot and bring to a boil. Place a 9-by 13-inch baking dish on the bottom rack of the oven. Now carefully pour the hot water into the pan. Make sure you have another rack centered in the middle of the oven.

6. Place the pie pan on a baking sheet. Pour the filling mixture into the pie crust. Loosely cover the edge of the pie with foil to shield the edge from becoming overly browned during baking.

7. Carefully place the pie on the baking sheet in the center of the middle oven rack directly over the water bath. Bake for 1 hour and 10 minutes. Turn off the oven but leave the pie in the oven for 10 more minutes. Do not open the oven door.

8. Remove the pie from the oven and place on a wire rack to completely cool. Does the ricotta pie need to be refrigerated? If you serve the pie the same day you make it, no. It can simply be served cooled at room temperature. Otherwise, cover the pie with plastic wrap and refrigerate for up to 3 days.

My dear friend Mehmet invited me to meet his favorite Turkish chef. We spent the entire day at Mehmet's home making an array of delicious Turkish pies. This recipe, for the unique Knafeh, is my favorite. I love the crunchiness of the kataifi, the sweetness of the sugar, lemon, rose water syrup, and the special sweet cheese in the center. The combination of flavors and creamy and crispy textures makes this pie a total delight. It's also an especially beautiful presentation with rose petals, pistachios, and a dusting of confectioners' sugar.

Knafeh

Makes approximately 12 to 14 individual knafeh

Prep Time: 45 minutes

Baking Time: 30 to 40 minutes plus 15 minutes to cool and 5 minutes to finish with syrup and pistachios

1 ¼ cups granulated sugar

1 ¼ cups water

½ teaspoon rose water

2 teaspoons lemon juice

18 tablespoons (9 ounces) unsalted butter, melted, divided

A few drops yellow gel food coloring, optional

16 ounces kataifi (shredded phyllo), thawed

14 to 16 ounces sweet cheese (see note)

2 cups coarsely crushed unsalted pistachios

Confectioners' sugar for dusting

Optional garnish: Edible rose petals

Note: A good substitute for sweet cheese is fresh mozzarella. Place the sliced mozzarella on a paper towel and press to remove excess liquid.

1. In a saucepan, combine the sugar and water. Heat on medium until the sugar is dissolved.

2. Remove the sugar syrup from the heat and let it cool for 5 minutes. Add the rose water and lemon juice. Set aside.

3. Preheat the oven to 350 degrees. In a small bowl, combine 2 tablespoons melted butter with a few drops of yellow gel food coloring, if using. I prepare these individual knafeh in muffin tins. Place the colored melted butter in the bottom of the muffin wells. Swirl the muffin tins to completely coat the bottom of the wells. Set aside.

4. Place the kataifi on a cutting board. Using a chef's knife, cut into ¼-inch pieces. Place the pieces in a large mixing bowl. Drizzle the remaining 16 tablespoons of melted butter over the kataifi. Mix gently until all the pieces are coated with butter.

5. Place two-thirds of the kataifi evenly in the muffin tins. Using the bottom of a small round glass, press the shredded kataifi firmly in the muffin wells so the mixture goes up the side of the wells. Use your fingers to work the kataifi so it completely covers the bottom and side of the muffin wells.

6. Slice the sweet cheese into thin small slices. Place the sliced cheese on top of the kataifi-lined muffin wells.

7. Press the remaining chopped kataifi on top of the cheese slices. Using your hands, press the kataifi layer down onto the cheese. Using a small offset spatula or the bottom of a small round glass, press gently on the edges to make sure the kataifi is firmly pressed around the entire circumference of the wells. *(continued)*

Knafeh

Continued

8. Place on a baking sheet. The butter often bubbles up as the knafeh bake, and the baking sheet will catch any overflow. Place in the preheated oven and bake for 30 to 40 minutes or until the shredded phyllo crust is golden brown and the butter is bubbling up the side of the muffin wells.

9. Remove from the oven and let cool for 15 minutes. Now you will need to flip the knafeh over onto a parchment-lined baking sheet. To do this take a paring knife and go around the circumference of the individual muffin wells to loosen the edges. Now place the parchment-lined baking sheet on top of the muffin tin. Quickly and carefully, flip the baking sheet so the muffin tin is now on top and the baking sheet on the bottom. Lift the muffin tin up. The bottom of the individual knafeh should now be on top!

10. Place some pistachios around the circumference of each knafeh. We will be pouring the rose water syrup on top of each miniature pie and the pistachios will serve as a dam to keep the syrup on the pie as it absorbs. Keep some pistachios to garnish the individual knafeh after the syrup is poured on top.

11. Using a spoon, carefully pour syrup over each knafeh. Work your way slowly to the edge, giving the syrup some time to soak into the phyllo crust. You may need to do this twice. If there is any additional syrup left, simply serve it on the side with the knafeh.

12. Once the syrup is absorbed, garnish the top of each knafeh with additional chopped pistachios and dust with confectioners' sugar. If using the rose petal garnish, do not add it to the top of the individual knafeh until you are ready to serve them. The knafeh are best served the day they are made, however they can be refrigerated for up to 3 days. Any longer and the phyllo will become too soft. I like to reheat the individual knafeh in the microwave for 30 seconds before serving.

In the past, this savory Easter pie from Liguria, Italy, was made with 33 sheets of thin pastry, one for each year of Jesus' life. (Don't worry, we are going to roll out only 4 sheets!) Grandmother Nerina, and mom, always told me to eat my greens and my home-grown Swiss chard has been a perfect addition to this spectacular pie. Although a family tradition, my friend Alejandra renewed my love for it. It's a popular dish in her native Argentina. The whole cooked eggs baked inside are essential. You can, however, substitute spinach or asparagus for the Swiss chard.

Torta Pasqualina

Makes 1 torta in a 9-inch springform pan or 10 by 13-inch deep terrine

Prep Time: 2 hours (includes making the crust and filling)

Baking Time: 55 to 65 minutes

Dough

3 cups plus 2 tablespoons all-purpose flour

1 cup cool water

1 teaspoon salt

¼ cup extra-virgin olive oil

Filling

2½ pounds Swiss chard, washed thoroughly and dried with paper towels

2 tablespoons extra-virgin olive oil plus additional for brushing between the dough layers

1 medium onion, chopped

2 garlic cloves, minced

9 large eggs, divided

1 cup whole milk ricotta cheese, drained in a colander for 30 minutes

½ cup firmly packed grated mozzarella

¼ cup grated Pecorino Romano

¼ cup grated Parmesan

1 tablespoon minced Italian parsley

A generous pinch of ground nutmeg, optional

Salt and black pepper to taste

Egg Wash

1 large egg

1 tablespoon cream

1. Place the flour in a large mixing bowl. In a separate bowl, stir together the water, salt, and oil. Pour the water mixture over the flour and mix until the dough comes together in a rough ball. Turn dough out onto a lightly floured work surface. Knead dough until smooth. Form the dough into a ball and, using the palm of your hand, flatten it into a disk. While the dough is resting, prepare the filling.

2. Strip the leaves of the chard from the thick stems. Stems and leaves will be cooked in different batches as the stems take longer to cook. Fill a large deep saucepan with water to a depth of approximately 2 to 3 inches. Bring water to a boil. Working in batches, add the Swiss chard leaves. Cover the pot with a lid and boil for 3 minutes or until tender. Remove the leaves using a slotted spoon and transfer to a large colander placed over a mixing bowl. Chop the stems and add them to the boiling water. Cook for approximately 5 to 7 minutes or until tender. Remove with a slotted spoon and place in the colander with the leaves.

3. Run cold water over Swiss chard to cool. Using your hands, squeeze out the excess water from the Swiss chard. Place on a cutting board and roughly chop. You will have approximately 4 cups of chopped leaves and stems. Place in a large mixing bowl.

4. Heat 2 tablespoons of olive oil in a large saucepan over medium heat. Sauté onions until soft and golden, about 4 to 5 minutes. Add the garlic and cook, stirring, for an additional minute. Add sautéed onions and garlic to the Swiss chard mixture.

5. In a separate mixing bowl, beat 4 of the eggs. Add the drained ricotta, mozzarella, Pecorino Romano, Parmesan, Swiss chard mixture, parsley, and nutmeg, if using. Stir to combine. Season with salt and black pepper to taste. *(continued)*

Torta Pasqualina

Continued

6. Preheat the oven to 375 degrees. Line a 9-inch springform pan with a round of parchment paper. If using a terrine pan, drape a piece of parchment paper over the sides of the pan so removal of the pie is easier. Now it's time to roll out the dough. Cut the dough disk into 4 pieces and form into balls. On a lightly floured work surface, roll out each ball into a thin 12-inch circle or rectangle. If you have difficulty rolling out the dough, try rolling it between 2 pieces of wax or parchment paper. You can stack the rolled-out dough on a baking sheet separating them with parchment or wax paper.

7. Carefully place 1 sheet of dough in the prepared pan. Lightly brush the top of the pastry with olive oil. Place a second sheet over the first. The dough will go over the edge of the pan. Use your fingers to gently adhere dough to the bottom and side of the pan.

8. Add the filling to the lined pan. There should be about a 2-inch thickness of filling. Smooth out the top of the filling using an offset spatula. Using the back of a spoon, make 5 indentations in the filling. Carefully crack an egg into each indentation.

9. Place a third sheet of dough over the top of the mixture and brush the top with olive oil. Place the last sheet of dough on top. Seal the pie by folding down the edge of the pastry lining to join with the top disk. Create a decorative edge by fluting the edge with your fingers. If you have extra dough, use it to cut out shapes to decorate the top of the torta.

10. In a small bowl, combine the remaining egg with the cream. Brush the top and edge of the pie with the egg wash. Using a paring knife, make 4 small steam vents on top of the pie. Place the filled pie on a baking sheet and bake for approximately 55 to 65 minutes or until the top is golden brown.

11. Remove pie from oven and place on a cooling rack. When cool enough to handle, remove the side of the pan and slide the pie onto a serving platter or cutting board. If using a terrine pan, use the parchment paper to lift the cooked pie out of the pan. Cool to room temperature before slicing. This pie is best served at room temperature.

I'm not sure, but I wouldn't be surprised if the first dessert I ever had was a cannoli. My grandmother made them often. When my extended family gets together these days, we don't ask if we want cannoli; we ask who is bringing the cannoli?! What makes this recipe special are the 3 cheeses: Ricotta, cream cheese, and mascarpone. If you don't like candied citron (I'm in your camp), candied orange peel can be used instead. Just don't forget the roasted pistachios on top!

Cannoli Pie

Makes one 9-inch pie

Prep Time: 40 minutes
Baking Time: 12 minutes
Chilling Time: 3 hours

Crust

14 ounces shelled pistachios

¼ cup granulated sugar

¼ cup firmly packed brown sugar

⅛ teaspoon salt

1 large egg

3 tablespoons unsalted butter, melted

Filling

1 (15 ounce) container ricotta cheese, strained

3 ounces cream cheese, room temperature

3 ounces mascarpone cheese, room temperature

1 cup sifted confectioners' sugar

½ teaspoon vanilla extract

6 ounces finely chopped bittersweet chocolate

2 tablespoons chopped candied orange peel, purchased or homemade, page 217

2 tablespoons chopped candied citron (optional)

Topping

¾ cup heavy whipping cream, chilled

4 ounces mascarpone cheese, room temperature

3 tablespoons confectioners' sugar

½ cup finely chopped roasted pistachios

Chocolate curls, page 220 or miniature chocolate chips

Candied orange peel

1. Preheat the oven to 350 degrees. Spray a 9-inch pie pan with nonstick cooking spray. In a food processor, combine the pistachios and sugars. Pulse until nuts are finely chopped. Add the remaining ingredients. Pulse several times until combined. Transfer the crust mixture to the prepared tart pan and, using your fingers, press firmly on the bottom and side of the pan. Refrigerate or freeze for 20 minutes. Place the lined pie pan on a baking sheet. Bake for 12 minutes. Remove and cool on a rack.

2. Place the ricotta cheese in a strainer over a bowl. Let sit for 20 minutes to remove any excess liquid.

3. In the bowl of a stand mixer, beat the cream cheese until fluffy, about 2 minutes. Scrape down the side of the bowl periodically. Add the strained ricotta and mix until creamy, about 2 more minutes. Now add the mascarpone, confectioners' sugar, and vanilla extract. Beat until combined. Using a spatula, fold in the chocolate, candied orange peel, and citron, if using. Transfer the filling into the cooled crust. Place the filled pie in the refrigerator while preparing the topping.

4. Place the heavy cream in the cleaned bowl attached to a stand mixer. Using the whip attachment, beat on medium high until soft peaks form. Add the room temperature mascarpone and the confectioners' sugar. Beat until just incorporated. It is important not to over whip the mascarpone or it can become grainy.

5. Place the whipped mascarpone cream on top of the pie. Sprinkle chopped pistachios, shaved chocolate, and candied orange peel on the cream topping. Chill for at least 3 hours before serving.

Our family always looks forward to Easter. It's the only time of year that my mom made her Easter Calzone, a recipe passed down from her own mother. The pie is full of delicious Italian meats and cheeses. My mom preferred to use Tuma cheese, a special Sicilian variety that is available just a few weeks out of the year at our family's favorite Italian deli. If you can't get your hands on Tuma, you can substitute Scamorza, unsalted mozzarella, or fresh provolone. I am so fortunate that my mom passed this recipe down to me. The tradition continues.

Easter Calzone
Makes one 10-inch pie using a cast iron skillet or 10-inch round baking dish

Prep Time: 45 minutes
Baking Time: 1 hour

Crust
4½ cups all-purpose flour, plus more as needed

2 teaspoons baking powder

1 teaspoon salt

1 cup (8 ounces) chilled unsalted butter, cut into pieces

3 large eggs, beaten

¾ cup milk

Filling
8 ounces prosciutto, cut into ¼-inch dice

1 pound cooked and crumbled ground mild Italian sausage

8 ounces soppressata, cut into ¼-inch dice

1 pound Tuma or Scamorza cheese, cut into ¼-inch dice (if not available, substitute provolone or mozzarella cheese)

½ cup grated Romano cheese

12 large eggs, beaten

1 teaspoon ground black pepper

Egg Glaze
1 large egg

1 tablespoon heavy cream

1. In the bowl of a food processor, combine the 4½ cups flour, baking powder, and salt. Pulse to combine. With the processor on, add the butter pieces through the feed tube a few at a time. Process until the mixture resembles coarse crumbs. Using the feed tube, slowly add beaten eggs followed by the milk. Process until a dough is formed. Transfer the dough to a lightly floured work surface. Gently work the dough with your hands until it becomes smooth. If the dough seems too wet, work in additional flour. Cover the dough with plastic wrap and let rest for 30 minutes.

2. In a large bowl, combine all of the meats, cheeses, 12 beaten eggs, and pepper. Set aside.

3. Preheat the oven to 375 degrees. Spray your baking dish or cast iron skillet with nonstick cooking spray. Divide the dough into 2 pieces. You will need two-thirds of the dough for the bottom and side of the pan and the remaining third for the top. On a lightly floured work surface, roll out the larger portion of dough into a 13-inch circle. Carefully transfer the rolled-out dough to your prepared pan. Using your fingers, press the dough into the pan bottom and side leaving a slight overhang.

4. Add the filling and smooth it out using an offset spatula.

5. Roll out the remaining piece of dough into an 11-inch circle. Moisten the edge of the overhang dough with water then set the rolled-out dough on top of the filled pan. Trim off edge excess and crimp the sides. Using a fork, prick several sets of holes across the top of the dough to allow steam to escape during baking. If you like, make decorative cutouts with any leftover dough to decorate the top of the pie.

6. Combine the egg and cream in a bowl. Brush the top of the pie pastry with the egg wash. If using decorative pastry cutouts, place them on top of the pastry now. Remember to brush the tops of the cutouts so they brown along with the pastry crust. Bake for approximately 1 hour or until the crust is nicely browned. Remove from the oven and cool on a rack. The pie needs to cool completely before serving.

Rice pudding is very popular throughout Latin America and Spain. I first tried this sweet comfort food in Argentina. It is easy to make and is best served chilled. I've been known to add a few raisins or pieces of candied lemon or orange peel, which adds another sweet and refreshing citrus note. For the crust, I like to use *speculoos* cookies, a crisp, brown, richly spiced short-crust variety from the Netherlands. Don't forget to add a dollop of whipped cream on top.

Arroz Con Leche Tartlets

Makes ten to twelve 4-inch tartlets

Prep Time: 1 hour
Baking Time: 10 minutes
Chilling Time: Minimum of 6 hours

Speculoos Cookie Crust

60 speculoos cookies
or
24 whole graham crackers
¾ cup (6 ounces) unsalted butter, melted
1 teaspoon ground cinnamon
(if using graham crackers)

Filling

3 tablespoons warm (110 degree) water
2 teaspoons unflavored Knox gelatin
¾ cup full-fat coconut milk
¾ cup whole milk
1½ cups heavy cream
⅔ cup granulated sugar, divided
2 tablespoons cornstarch
¼ teaspoon salt
2 large eggs
1½ cups (firmly packed) cooked short
or medium-grain rice

Salted Coconut Caramel

¾ cup full-fat coconut milk
½ cup firmly packed brown sugar
2 tablespoons cold unsalted butter,
cut into small pieces
½ teaspoon sea salt

Cinnamon Rum Whipped Cream

1¼ cups heavy whipping cream, chilled
2 tablespoons confectioners' sugar
1 tablespoon cornstarch
1 to 2 tablespoons dark rum (to taste)
½ teaspoon ground cinnamon

1. In the bowl of a food processor, pulse the cookies or graham crackers into fine crumbs. You should have about 1½ cups of crumbs. Add the melted butter and, if using, the cinnamon. Pulse in 10-second intervals until the mixture is combined. Press the mixture evenly into the base and side of ten to twelve 4-inch tartlet pans. Place lined tart pans in the refrigerator or freezer while preheating the oven to 350 degrees.

2. Bake the chilled lined tartlet pans until the crusts begin to darken slightly, about 8 to 10 minutes. Remove from the oven and let cool completely before filling.

3. In a small bowl, combine the warm water and gelatin. Mix to combine. Let the gelatin mixture rest and "bloom" while preparing the remaining filling.

4. In a heavy saucepan, combine the coconut milk, whole milk, cream, and ⅓ cup of the sugar. Heat on medium-high heat until simmering then reduce heat to medium low.

5. In a mixing bowl, combine the cornstarch, salt, and remaining ⅓ cup sugar. Whisk to combine. Add the eggs and continue to whisk until well combined. Now, slowly add half of the warm cream mixture, whisking constantly, to temper the egg mixture. Pour the egg mixture back into the pan with the cream and whisk to combine. Add the rice. Bring to a boil over medium heat, stirring constantly while scraping the bottom and side of the pan. Remove from the heat and stir in the gelatin. Transfer the mixture to a clean bowl and allow to cool to room temperature. Place plastic wrap over the mixture, pressing down so the wrap touches the filling. This will prevent a crust from forming. Chill overnight.

6. When ready to assemble, prepare the caramel. Place the remaining ¾ cup full-fat coconut milk and brown sugar in a heavy saucepan. Cook over medium heat, whisking constantly for 2 minutes. Reduce heat and cook, stirring often with a heat-proof spatula, until reduced to a thick sauce, about 10 to 15 minutes. Remove from the heat and whisk in the butter and salt. Pour the caramel evenly into the cooked tart shells, tilting as needed to cover the tart shell bottoms. Freeze for 15 minutes to set.

7. Fill the tartlet shells with the chilled rice filling. I like to mound quite a bit of filling into each tart shell. Chill 2 hours or overnight. When ready to serve, prepare the rum cream. Place the cream in a chilled bowl of a stand mixer. Using the whip attachment, whip the cream on medium-high speed until soft peaks form. Reduce speed to medium and slowly add the confectioners' sugar followed by the cornstarch, rum, and cinnamon. I usually add 1 tablespoon of rum to start then add additional to taste. Whip until firm peaks form. Mound the whipped cream on top of each tartlet. Serve with any remaining caramel sauce. You won't want any to go to waste!

Pasta Frola is a type of sweet tart common to Argentina. It's essentially a short crust slathered with a delicious jam. For the jam, I like to use quince (also known as membrillo), which is a cousin of apples and pears. In this traditional recipe, the paste is crumbled and melted with orange juice and dulce de leche. I finish the tart with a traditional lattice crust so the jam shines through. To make the tart extra special, I add a glaze of apricot preserves flavored with orange liqueur.

Pasta Frola (Quince Tart)

Makes one 8-inch tart

Prep Time: 60 minutes
Baking Time: 40 to 45 minutes

Dough

3½ cups all-purpose flour
2 teaspoons baking powder
½ teaspoon salt
¾ cup granulated sugar
Zest of 1 orange
¾ cup (6 ounces) unsalted butter
1 teaspoon vanilla extract
2 large egg yolks
1 large egg
½ cup whole milk, as needed

Filling

12 ounces quince paste cut into cubes and crumbled into small pieces
3 tablespoons orange juice
½ cup dulce de leche, purchased or make your own, page 219

Egg Wash, Apricot Glaze, and Garnish

1 egg
1 tablespoon cream
½ cup apricot preserves
1 tablespoon orange-flavored liqueur
Confectioners' sugar

1. In the bowl of a food processor, combine the flour, baking powder, salt, sugar, and orange zest. Pulse to combine. With the processor on, slowly add the cubed cold butter through the feed tube, pulsing to incorporate. Add the vanilla, egg yolks, and egg through the feed tube and pulse to incorporate. Add ¼ cup milk through the feed tube and pulse to incorporate. If the pastry does not come together, add the additional ¼ cup of milk as needed. Remove the dough from the food processor and form into a ball. Using the palm of your hand, press the dough to form a disk. Wrap with plastic wrap and refrigerate for 30 minutes.

2. Using your fingers, crumble the quince paste cubes. Place the crumbled quince paste, orange juice, and dulce de leche in a heavy saucepan. On low heat, cook the mixture, stirring constantly with a heat-proof spatula, until the quince paste melts and incorporates with the dulce de leche to form a smooth paste. Remove from heat.

3. Spray an 8-inch tart pan with a removable bottom with nonstick cooking spray. Line the pan bottom with parchment paper. Lightly flour your work surface. Portion the chilled dough into a ⅔ portion and a ⅓ portion. The larger portion will be used to line the tart pan and the smaller portion for the lattice top decoration.

4. Preheat the oven to 350 degrees. Roll the larger portion of dough into a 10-inch circle or square. Transfer the dough to the prepared pan and gently press it in the bottom and side of the pan. Use a rolling pin or sharp knife to trim the dough flush with the pan side. Refrigerate or freeze the dough-lined pan for 15 minutes.

5. Using a spatula, transfer the quince filling evenly into the tart pan. On a lightly floured work surface, roll out the remaining dough into a 9-inch square or round. Cut the dough into ½-inch strips. Place the strips in a lattice design on top of the tart. For more information on creating a lattice design, see page 28. *(continued)*

Pasta Frola (Quince Tart)
Continued

6. In a small bowl, beat together the egg and the cream. Using a pastry brush, glaze the lattice top with the egg wash. Set the tart on a baking sheet and bake for 40 to 45 minutes or until the lattice crust is nicely browned.

7. Towards the end of baking, prepare the apricot glaze. In a small saucepan, melt the apricot preserves with the orange liqueur. Place the melted preserves in a small mesh strainer that has been placed over a small bowl. Using the back of a spoon, press the apricot mixture through the sieve.

8. Remove the tart from the oven and immediately brush the apricot glaze on the warm lattice crust. Let the tart cool for 30 minutes then remove the tart pan side and transfer to a serving platter. Dust the top of the tart with confectioners' sugar. The tart can be served slightly warm or at room temperature.

These puckery lemon hand pies were a favorite in high school. My first "real" job was at Arthur Treacher's Fish & Chips, which served a fried version of this delectable treat. I make the recipe a bit easier by baking the individual pies.

These little pies are best when made with homemade lemon curd. Prepare it ahead so the filling can cool before putting together the pies. When the urge strikes and I'm pressed for time, I use a 15-ounce can of lemon pie filling and two packages of refrigerated pie crust.

Lemon Love Hand Pies

Makes approximately 8 pies

Prep Time: 40 minutes
Baking Time: 20 to 25 minutes

Crust
Mary's Favorite Pie Dough, page 30

Egg Wash
1 large egg
2 tablespoons heavy cream

Filling
1½ cups lemon curd, purchased or homemade, page 216

Optional Toppings
Confectioners' sugar
Demerara sugar
Confectioners' sugar glaze (1½ cups sifted confectioners' sugar mixed with 1 to 2 tablespoons water)
Melted white chocolate

1. On a lightly floured work surface, roll out one half of the dough to a thickness of approximately ¼-inch. Using a 3½-inch round cookie cutter, cut the dough into 8 rounds. Set the cut pieces on a parchment-lined baking sheet. Dust your surface again with flour and roll out the remaining piece of dough. Cut the same number of pieces but keep them on your work board.

2. Spread approximately 1 heaping tablespoon of the lemon curd filling onto the center of the pastry pieces that are on the baking sheet, keeping a ⅛-inch edge free of filling. In a small bowl, combine the egg with the heavy cream. Using a pastry brush, lightly brush the side of the lemon curd filled pastry. Keep the remaining egg wash to brush the top of the pies right before baking them. Now take the pastry pieces that are on your work surface and place them on top of the lemon curd. Using the tines of a fork, crimp the dough sides so both pieces adhere. Place the baking sheet in the refrigerator for at least 30 minutes. If you have leftover lemon curd, simply place it in a container and refrigerate for later use. It is terrific on toast or an English muffin!

3. When ready to bake the pies, preheat the oven to 375 degrees. Brush the top of the pies with the remaining egg wash. Bake until the pies are a nice golden brown, about 20 to 25 minutes.

4. Now it's time to finish the pies with one (or all!) of the suggested toppings. Once the pies are slightly cooled, sprinkle them with confectioners' sugar or raw sugar. If you want to get extra fancy, you can drizzle the pies with a confectioners' sugar glaze or melted white chocolate.

Pies at the Farm

I am lucky to have a farm in Central Illinois—it's my happy place. Life is good on the farm with seasonal fruits and vegetables ready to pick right off the tree, vine, and stem.

Nothing is better than visiting my neighbors in the country and having them insist on sending me home with a bushel of this or that. And of course it's impossible to resist stopping at roadside produce stands. I've been known to buy vegetables directly from the back of pickup trucks! Pure heaven.

There's also plenty of fresh fish on the farm from stocked lakes, as well as a bounty of various meats. As a result of my husband's love of hunting, we enjoy a constant and bountiful supply of game including elk, venison, duck, and pheasant.

The farm is where I relax and don't get fussy about food. Homespun pies like my apple blackberry pandowdy and strawberry rhubarb are farm staples. My honey pie puts the honey from my beekeeper neighbor to good use and makes my husband, Billy, happy. And that bounty from Billy's hunting gets transformed into the most delicious hunter's pie.

You may not have a farm, but you probably have a local farmers market that can provide you with most of the ingredients in this chapter. I urge you to relax a bit when making these pies. The recipes are designed to bring out the best of those fresh ingredients with an emphasis on taste, not looks!

Mary's tip: Use ground meat
instead of cubed, which can dry out
during cooking and lack tenderness.
The addition of juniper berries,
crushed with the back of a chef's
knife, is well worth trying.
This savory comfort food is
a sure-fire crowd-pleaser.

Ⓜ

My husband is an avid hunter, so my freezer is packed with seasonal elk, deer, duck, and pheasant. It was only natural to create a pie featuring, in this case, elk and duck. Both meats are low in fat and can be tough if overcooked. I like to serve those hungry hunters a large casserole of this pie, but you can also make individual servings, just like individual pot pies!

Billy's Hunter Pie

Makes one 2-quart casserole or sixteen 1-cup individual servings

Prep Time: 1½ hours
Cooking Time: 1 hour 50 minutes

Stew Filling
6 pieces applewood-smoked bacon, diced
6 duck legs
Salt and pepper
5 shallots, peeled and quartered
1 tablespoon sugar
3 tablespoons unsalted butter
½ cup all-purpose flour
3 cups full-bodied red wine
2½ cups beef stock, plus more as needed
3 tablespoons tomato paste
1 tablespoon chopped fresh thyme leaves
or
1 teaspoon dried thyme
4 juniper berries, crushed, optional
1 tablespoon olive oil
1½ pounds ground venison or elk
2 garlic cloves, minced
2 cups washed unpeeled red potatoes, cut into ½-inch dice
2 cups peeled carrots, cut into ¼-inch dice
2 tablespoons cornstarch dissolved in ¼ cup water, as needed to thicken the sauce
2 tablespoons chopped Italian parsley

Pastry Top
1 to 2 sheets frozen puff pastry, thawed according to directions
1 large egg
1 tablespoon heavy cream

1. Preheat the oven to 350 degrees. In a large 2-quart Dutch oven, cook the bacon on medium heat until crisp. Remove the bacon and keep 1 tablespoon of the fat in the pot. Discard the remaining fat or keep for a later use.

2. Season the duck legs with salt and pepper. Reheat the pot used for the bacon. Carefully place the duck legs in the pot so they lay flat. Once the duck legs begin to brown, turn them over to cook the other side. You may need to do this in batches. Remove the duck legs and place on a paper towel-lined platter. Discard all but 1 tablespoon of the fat.

3. In the same pot on medium heat, sauté the quartered shallots until lightly browned. Sprinkle with the sugar and continue to cook until golden in color. Remove the shallots from the pot.

4. Melt the butter in the Dutch oven. Stir in the flour and cook, stirring constantly, for 1 minute. Now add the red wine, beef stock, and tomato paste along with the thyme and juniper berries, if using. Return the bacon and duck legs to the Dutch oven. If the duck legs are not completely covered, add just enough additional beef stock to cover them. Cover and place in the preheated oven for 1 hour.

5. While the duck legs are braising in the oven, cook the ground venison or elk. In a clean skillet, heat 1 tablespoon of olive oil. Add the ground venison or elk and cook on medium heat until cooked through. Add the garlic and cook for 30 seconds. Set aside.

6. After 1 hour of braising, add the potatoes and carrots to the Dutch oven. Re-cover and return to the oven for another 20 to 25 minutes or until the duck is tender and the potatoes are fork tender.

7. Remove from the oven and carefully lift the duck legs out of the Dutch oven. Place on a platter. When cool enough to handle, discard the duck skin, and remove the duck meat from the bones. The meat should be rather chunky. You can use a knife to cut it into smaller pieces if you like. Discard the skin and bones. *(continued)*

Billy's Hunter Pie

Continued

8. Place the duck meat, along with the reserved ground venison and shallots, into the Dutch oven. If you would like a thicker sauce, place the Dutch oven on a burner on medium heat. Be careful touching the Dutch oven in case it is still hot. When the mixture comes to a simmer, drizzle in enough of the cornstarch and water mixture to create the sauce consistency you would like. Stir in the chopped Italian parsley and taste for salt and pepper. Season as needed.

9. Increase the oven temperature to 375 degrees. Let the stew cool 15 minutes before finishing with the puff pastry top. The stew should be warm but not too hot or the pastry will soften too much before it hits the heat of the oven. Transfer the mixture to a 2-quart casserole dish or divide among individual oven-safe mini-casserole dishes. The stew should come up to about ½ inch from the top of the dish.

10. Cut out a piece of puff pastry about 2 inches larger than the baking dish. Depending on the size of the baking dish, you may need 2 sheets of puff pastry. If using individual dishes, cut the pastry into rounds or squares that are 1-inch larger than the top of the dish. Combine the egg and cream in a small bowl. Place the pastry on top of the stew. Using your hands, gently press the pastry so it adheres to the side of the dish. Brush the pastry top with the egg wash mixture. Place the baking dish or individual baking dishes on a baking sheet to catch any of the stew that may bubble over.

11. Bake for 20 to 22 minutes or until the pastry is golden brown. Serve immediately.

Nothing says farm-style breakfast like corned beef hash and eggs. Plus, I love using leftovers! My recipe is the perfect landing place for leftover corned beef, but feel free to use roast beef, ham, sausage, or chicken. For the crispiest hash, use a large skillet so the hash doesn't stick to the pan and don't flip the hash too soon. In our family, it's not breakfast without eggs just the way you like them. Eggs paired with this hash, well, breakfast just doesn't get any better.

Corned Beef Hash Breakfast Tarts

Makes 8 individual tarts

Prep Time: 40 minutes if making your own hash

Baking Time: 15 minutes

Corned Beef

3 tablespoons unsalted butter

1 cup chopped onion

3 cups finely chopped cooked corned beef

3 cups chopped peeled and cooked Yukon gold potatoes

2 tablespoons chopped Italian parsley

Salt and ground black pepper to taste

Breakfast Tarts

1 recipe corned beef

2 sheets of frozen puff pastry, thawed

1½ cups shredded Swiss cheese

8 large eggs

Salt and ground black pepper to taste

Sriracha sauce to taste

1. In a large skillet on medium heat, melt the butter. Add the onions and cook for 2 to 3 minutes, or until translucent.

2. Add the corned beef and potatoes and mix gently to combine. Spread the mixture out evenly over the pan. Increase the heat to medium high and press the mixture down with a spatula.

3. Do not stir the potatoes and corned beef. Let them brown on their own. Use a spatula to peek under a small section of the mixture to see if it is nice and brown. When ready, use a metal spatula to flip the mixture. I find it easiest to flip the mixture in sections.

4. Press the mixture down again and brown the other side of the potatoes and corned beef. When the mixture is browned, add the parsley and season with salt and pepper to taste. It is fine to stir the mixture, but only after both sides have crisped and browned. The hash can be cooled and stored in the refrigerator or can be made into the breakfast tarts right away.

5. Preheat the oven to 400 degrees. Line 2 baking sheets with parchment paper.

6. On a lightly floured work surface, place 1 sheet of the puff pastry. Roll out the pastry into an 11 by 11-inch square. Cut it into 4 squares. Place the squares on one of the prepared pans and continue the same process with the remaining piece of puff pastry.

7. Divide the cooled corned beef among the pastry squares, leaving a ½-inch border around the edge. Divide the Swiss cheese evenly over the hash. Using your fingers, form a round indentation in the center of each tart. This is where the egg will go.

8. Carefully crack an egg into the center of each square. Sprinkle lightly with salt and pepper. Bake until the eggs are cooked but yolks are still a bit runny, about 12 to 15 minutes depending on your egg preference.

9. Remove and place on a serving platter or individual plates. Drizzle lightly with Sriracha sauce to taste.

Pandowdy, a favorite of mine, is an American classic from the 1800s that got its name from the messy or "dowdy" way the pieces of crust are arranged atop the fruit mixture. This twist on apple pie is baked in a cast iron skillet. I add blackberries and serve the finished pandowdy warm with a mound of vanilla ice cream. I once came upon my young daughters gathered over my pandowdy, spoons poised. The next morning, I looked for leftovers to enjoy with coffee. No luck, no problem. It's easy to make. I just made another.

Apple Blackberry Pandowdy

Makes one 9-inch cast iron skillet pie

Prep Time: 40 minutes

Baking Time: 30 to 35 minutes

Crust

1 cup all-purpose flour

½ teaspoon salt

½ teaspoon sugar

¼ teaspoon cinnamon

½ cup (4 ounces) unsalted butter, cold, cut into small cubes

3 to 4 tablespoons ice water

Filling

2 pounds (8 cups sliced), Granny Smith or Honeycrisp apples, peeled and sliced

1 tablespoon fresh lemon juice

¼ cup all-purpose flour

⅔ cup firmly packed brown sugar

1 teaspoon cinnamon

¼ teaspoon ground nutmeg

⅛ teaspoon salt

4 tablespoons (2 ounces) unsalted butter, cut into cubes

½ cup apple juice (more if needed)

1 pint fresh blackberries, rinsed and patted dry

Garnish

1 large egg

1 tablespoon cream

Demerara or raw sugar

1. In the bowl of a food processor, combine the flour, salt, sugar, and cinnamon. Pulse to blend. Using the feed tube, add the butter cubes, a few at a time, pulsing the processor as you add them. The mixture should resemble coarse sand when all the butter is incorporated. With the processor on, slowly drizzle in the ice-cold water, 1 tablespoon at a time, until the mixture comes together. You may not need all the water.

2. Turn the dough out on a lightly floured work surface and press together into a disc. Wrap in plastic wrap and chill in the refrigerator for 1 hour.

3. Preheat the oven to 425 degrees. Place the peeled, sliced apples and lemon juice in a bowl and toss to combine.

4. In a separate bowl, combine the flour, brown sugar, spices, and salt. Sprinkle this mixture on top of the apples and mix gently to combine.

5. In a 9-inch cast iron skillet, melt the remaining 4 tablespoons of butter. Add the apple mixture and cook for 2 minutes, stirring often, to soften the apples. Add ½ cup of apple juice and stir to combine. Continue to simmer the mixture until the liquid gets thick and starts to stick to the pan. Please note, if the mixture seems too thick, feel free to drizzle in a little more apple juice as needed.

6. On a lightly floured work surface, roll the pie dough into a 12-inch square. Cut into 2-inch squares. It's ok if they are not perfect!

7. Sprinkle the fresh blackberries on top of the apples in the cast iron pan. Place the pastry squares around the top of the skillet, leaving some space between the squares so the mixture "bubbles up" over the crust as it bakes.

8. In a small bowl, whisk together the egg and cream. Using a pastry brush, lightly glaze the top of the pastry squares with the egg mixture. Sprinkle with the raw sugar. Place the cast iron pan on a baking sheet. The pan will catch any juices that may boil over during baking. Bake for 30 to 35 minutes or until the top crust is a deep golden brown and the fruit mixture starts to bubble over the crust slightly.

9. Remove from the oven and let cool on a rack for 15 minutes. Scoop the pandowdy into serving bowls and serve with a generous scoop of vanilla ice cream.

Growing up Italian, it's no surprise I love tomatoes, cheese, and basil. This recipe includes a buttery French crust called *pâte brisée* and heirloom tomatoes. Most heirlooms originated before 1951 and some are over 100 years old. Because heirlooms are open pollinated, they are disease-resistant but also don't keep as long as their hybrid cousins. When I am fortunate enough to find these beauties, I make this recipe. The colorful heirloom tomatoes make a stunning presentation and one delicious tart.

Heirloom Tomato and Basil Tart

Makes one 9-inch tart

Prep Time: 35 minutes
Baking Time: 55 minutes

Crust

½ recipe Pâte Brisée, page 31
or
½ recipe Mary's Favorite Pie Dough, page 30

Tart Filling

2 to 3 large heirloom tomatoes

12 smaller teardrop tomatoes, various colors, cut in half

2 teaspoons extra-virgin olive oil

2 shallots, peeled and minced

1 garlic clove, minced

4 large eggs

1 cup half and half

¼ teaspoon dried oregano

½ teaspoon salt

A pinch of white pepper

3 tablespoons chopped basil leaves

1½ cups grated mozzarella or provolone (or a combination!)

Garnish

2 tablespoons thinly sliced basil leaves

1. Line a 9-inch tart pan with a removable bottom with a round of parchment paper. Lightly spray the pan bottom and side with nonstick cooking spray. Lightly flour your work surface and roll the dough into a 12-inch circle. Drape the dough gently in the pan. Using your fingers, press the dough into the bottom and side of the pan. Use a rolling pin or sharp knife to trim the dough flush with the pan side. Refrigerate or freeze the dough-lined pan for 30 minutes.

2. Preheat the oven to 350 degrees. Cut the large heirloom tomatoes into ¼-inch slices. Place the tomato slices and teardrop tomato halves on a paper towel-lined baking sheet. Place additional paper towels on top and press gently. The paper towels will absorb excess water from the tomatoes.

3. Remove the lined tart pan from the freezer or refrigerator. We will be partially baking the crust before filling the tart. Line the chilled tart shell with parchment paper. Fill with pie weights or dried beans. Make sure the weights are evenly distributed around the pan bottom. Bake until the edge of the crust begins to brown, about 12 minutes. Remove from the oven and carefully lift the parchment paper (with the weights) out of the tart pan. Bake for an additional 4 minutes. The bottom crust will be light brown but not cooked through. Remove from the oven and let cool on a rack for 15 minutes before filling the tart. For more information on blind baking a crust, see page 29.

4. In a small sauté pan, heat the olive oil on medium heat. Add the shallots and garlic. Sauté for 1 minute until just translucent. Remove from heat.

5. In a mixing bowl, combine the eggs, half and half, oregano, salt, and white pepper. Stir in 3 tablespoons of the chopped fresh basil. Place the tart pan on a baking sheet. Spread the shallot garlic mixture on the bottom of the tart shell. Place half of the heirloom tomatoes on top of the shallots, interspersing half of the smaller tomato halves between the larger slices. Sprinkle evenly with half of the cheese. Gently pour the egg mixture into the tart pan. Sprinkle remaining cheese on top of the egg mixture.

6. Arrange the remaining heirloom tomatoes on top of the tart, interspersing the smaller tomato halves between the larger slices. Bake in the preheated oven until the tart is set, about 40 minutes. Remove and let rest for 5 minutes. Carefully lift the tart out of the pan. Sprinkle the remaining fresh basil on top.

When my children were young, we'd pick plenty of Granny Smith apples at a local orchard to make the perfect apple pie. Firm enough to hold up to the heat of baking, Granny Smiths also complement warm autumn spices such as cinnamon and nutmeg. A generous family friend who makes this delicious pie shared the recipe, called "slab" because it's made in a large baking sheet. I usually make two! One I bake right away and the other I freeze unbaked ready for future get-togethers.

Apple Slab Pie
Makes one 9 by 13-inch slab pie

Prep Time: 45 minutes
Baking Time: 1 hour

Crust
4½ cups all-purpose flour
1 teaspoon salt
1½ cups Crisco™ shortening
3 large egg yolks
2½ tablespoons fresh lemon juice
½ cup plus 3 tablespoons cold water

Filling
4 pounds Granny Smith apples
2 tablespoons all-purpose flour
1 cup granulated sugar
1½ teaspoons ground cinnamon
½ teaspoon ground nutmeg

Optional Glaze
2 cups confectioners' sugar
2 to 3 tablespoons water

1. In a mixing bowl, sift together the flour and salt. Using a pastry blender, cut the shortening into the flour. In a separate bowl, whisk the egg yolks slightly. Add the lemon juice and the water. Slowly add this mixture to the flour and salt, stirring until a dough forms. Form the dough into a ball then flatten into a disk using the palm of your hand. Wrap in plastic wrap and refrigerate while preparing the apple filling. The dough can also be prepared in a food processor.

2. Peel and core the apples. Cut into ¼-inch slices and place in a mixing bowl. Add the flour, sugar, cinnamon, and nutmeg and toss gently to combine.

3. Preheat the oven to 350 degrees. Remove the dough from the refrigerator and divide it in half. On a lightly floured work surface, roll one half of the dough into a 10 by 15-inch rectangle. Place the dough into a 9 by 13-inch baking sheet that has been sprayed with nonstick cooking spray. The dough edge should drape over the sides of the sheet.

4. Roll the remaining piece of dough into the same sized rectangle. Transfer the apple mixture into the dough-lined pan, spreading the mixture evenly. Top with the other piece of dough. Trim the dough edge as needed then use the tines of a fork to seal the edge. Alternatively, you can make the pie more dramatic by putting a lattice crust with leaf cutouts on top of the slab pie. See page 28 for instructions.

5. Place the pan on a baking sheet. The pan will catch any apple juice that may bubble over during the baking process. Bake for 1 hour or until the pastry is a rich brown color.

6. Cool completely before slicing. If you prepared the pie using a single top crust, I like to drizzle the optional confectioners' sugar glaze on top of the cooled pie. If you prepared the slab pie using a lattice design and cutouts, it's your choice if you want to glaze the top. To prepare the glaze, place the confectioners' sugar in a bowl. Add enough of the water to create a nice glaze consistency. Using a fork, drizzle the glaze on top of the pastry. Slice the cooled apple-filled pastry into bars.

Summer at the farm brings bushels of fresh vegetables ripe for savory creations. This sweet corn and zucchini pie is a favorite. A snap to put together, I bake it in my trusty cast iron skillet. The pie has no crust, so the whole family can dive in—including my daughter who enjoys a gluten-free diet. For consistent, thin slices of zucchini, use a handheld mandoline slicer. A simple piece of parchment paper lines the skillet, making it easy to remove the pie from the pan to a cutting board or serving platter. Growing up, my mom made this pie and it was so tasty we almost forgot we were eating vegetables! I add mushrooms and cheese to round out the deliciousness. I know mom would approve.

Farmhouse Corn and Zucchini Pie

Makes one 9-inch pie

Prep Time: 35 minutes
Baking Time: 25 minutes

4 cups very thinly sliced zucchini
(about 2 large zucchini)

4 tablespoons (2 ounces) unsalted butter

½ cup finely chopped onion

8 ounces sliced cremini or shiitake
mushrooms

1½ cups fresh sweet corn
(about 2 to 3 ears)

6 ounces shredded mozzarella cheese

6 ounces shredded Swiss or white cheddar
cheese

1 tablespoon freshly chopped basil
or 1 teaspoon dried basil

1 tablespoon freshly chopped oregano
or 1 teaspoon dried oregano

½ teaspoon salt

⅛ teaspoon pepper

5 large eggs, beaten

1. Preheat the oven to 375 degrees. Cut a 14-inch circle of parchment paper. Line a 10-inch cast iron skillet with the parchment circle. Spray the parchment with nonstick cooking spray. If you don't have a cast iron pan, simply use a 9-inch-deep dish pie pan. Set aside.

2. Remove 8 zucchini slices. These will be used to top the pie before it is baked. In a medium sauté pan, melt the butter on medium heat. Add the onions, remaining zucchini, and mushrooms. Sauté until the vegetables begin to soften, about 5 minutes. Add the corn kernels and continue to sauté for about 2 to 3 more minutes. Transfer the mixture to a mixing bowl to cool.

3. Reserve about ¼ cup of either type of cheese to place on top of the pie. Add the remaining cheese, basil, oregano, salt, pepper, and eggs to the cooled vegetable mixture. Transfer the mixture to the prepared pan. Decorate the top of the pie with the reserved zucchini slices then sprinkle with the ¼ cup of the reserved cheese.

4. Place the cast iron skillet on a baking sheet. The pan will catch any of the mixture that may boil over and make removing the pan from the oven easier. Cover the pie loosely with foil that has been sprayed with nonstick cooking spray. Bake for 20 minutes, then remove the foil and bake for an additional 5 minutes to brown the top. Remove from the oven and let rest, in the pan, for 15 minutes. For a crispier top, place under the broiler for about 1 minute, making sure it's not too close so the paper doesn't burn. Use the parchment paper to lift the pie out of the cast iron pan and place it on a cutting board or serving platter. Slice, serve, and enjoy!

Strawberries and rhubarb go together, an enticing balance of sweet and tart. Rhubarb season is short so load up at the grocery store or farmers market! I make this pie with either a double-crust or a lattice top. Give the pie crust a good sprinkle of coarse sugar on top before baking. It melts just a bit, retaining its texture and giving the pie crust just the right amount of sweet crunch. If you want to go over the top with this one, serve with a generous dollop of honey-flavored whipped cream.

Strawberry Rhubarb Pie

Makes one double-crust or lattice 9-inch pie

Prep Time: 45 minutes

Baking Time: 1 hour

Crust

Mary's Favorite Pie Dough, page 30

Filling

4 cups (1 pound) washed rhubarb, cut into ½-inch pieces

2½ cups strawberries (1.25 pounds) sliced

⅓ cup granulated sugar

⅓ cup firmly packed light brown sugar

¼ cup cornstarch

¼ teaspoon salt

1 tablespoon freshly squeezed lemon juice

1 teaspoon orange zest

½ teaspoon ground cardamom (this is optional, but I really love this flavor addition!)

Pastry Glaze

1 large egg

1 tablespoon cream

Demerara or raw sugar

Honey Whipped Cream, optional

1½ cups heavy cream, chilled

5 tablespoons honey

1. Lightly dust your work surface with flour and roll out 1 disk of dough into an 11-inch round. Save the remaining dough disk to make the pie top. Spray a 9-inch pie pan with nonstick cooking spray. Place the dough round in the prepared pan. Using kitchen scissors, trim the edge of the dough, leaving ¾-inch of overhang. Refrigerate or freeze while preparing the filling.

2. Preheat the oven to 400 degrees. In a large mixing bowl combine the rhubarb, strawberries, sugars, cornstarch, salt, lemon juice, orange zest, and optional cardamom. Toss gently to combine.

3. Remove the lined pie pan from the refrigerator or freezer. Spoon the filling into the prepared crust. I favor using a slotted spoon to do this. You want to place the filling in the pie shell but not the excess liquid. If there is excess liquid left in your mixing bowl, discard it.

4. Now it's time to put the "top" on the pie. Roll out the remaining piece of pie dough. You can either make a double-crust pie, or finish the pie with a lattice design. If using a double-crust, roll out the remaining piece of dough into a 10-inch circle. Using your rolling pin, carefully roll up the pastry. Place the rolling pin on one side of your filled pie and gently unroll the dough so it is on top of the pie. An easy tip but it works every time! Trim off any excess dough and flute or crimp the edges. Using a paring knife, carefully make 3 slits in the center of the pie so steam can be released during baking. You can also cut out a design on the top crust like I did in my photo or make a lattice crust. Refer to my directions on how to weave and finish the lattice crust on page 28.

5. In a small bowl, combine the egg and cream. Brush the top pastry or lattice with the egg wash and sprinkle generously with the demerara or raw sugar.

6. Place the pie on a baking sheet. The baking sheet will catch any excess that may ooze out of the pie during the baking process. Bake on the middle rack of the oven for 20 minutes. Reduce the oven temperature to 350 degrees and continue to bake pie for 40 to 45 minutes or until the pie crust is nicely browned. Allow the pie to cool on a rack at room temperature for at least 3 hours before slicing.

7. When ready to serve, prepare the whipped cream. Place the cream in a chilled bowl of a stand mixer. Using the whip attachment, whip the cream on medium-high speed until soft peaks form. Reduce speed to medium and slowly add the honey. Whip until medium firm peaks form. Serve immediately with the strawberry rhubarb pie.

Hummingbirds love our farm and the feeling is mutual. The tiny birds hover at dawn and dusk as they enjoy sweet nectars. It's magical. Hummingbirds remind me of a southern favorite, hummingbird cake. My hummingbird pie transforms this classic into pie form with a filling of pineapple, bananas, and, in my interpretation, dried apricots. The topping of coconut and pecan crumble finishes off this new classic dessert. Your family and guests will flock to this pie as do hummingbirds to the sweet nectar of a flower!

Hummingbird Pie

Makes one 9-inch pie

Prep Time: 45 minutes
Baking Time: 40 minutes
Rest Time: 6 hours or overnight

Crust

½ recipe Pâte Brisée, page 31
or
½ recipe Mary's Favorite Pie Dough, page 30

Crumble Topping

¼ cup whole rolled oats, not instant
½ cup all-purpose flour
¼ cup firmly packed light brown sugar
1 teaspoon ground cinnamon
½ teaspoon ground ginger
Pinch of salt
6 tablespoons (3 ounces) unsalted butter, melted
½ cup pecan pieces
½ cup coconut flakes

Filling

½ cup firmly packed light brown sugar
3 tablespoons cornstarch
¼ teaspoon ground nutmeg
1 teaspoon ground cinnamon
1 tablespoon finely chopped crystallized ginger
⅛ teaspoon salt
2½ cups of finely chopped fresh pineapple
2 ripe bananas, peeled and cut into ¼-inch slices
½ cup diced dried apricots
1 teaspoon fresh lemon juice
1 tablespoon spiced rum, optional

Garnish

Vanilla ice cream
Honey caramel sauce, page 223

1. Lightly dust your work surface with flour and roll the dough into an 11-inch round. Spray a 9-inch pie pan with nonstick cooking spray. Place the dough round in the prepared pan. Using kitchen scissors, trim the edge of the dough, leaving ¾-inch of overhang. Crimp or flute the side of the dough and refrigerate or freeze for 30 minutes.

2. Prepare the crumble topping. Place the oats in the bowl of a food processor and pulse until they resemble coarse cornmeal.

3. In a bowl, combine the oats, flour, brown sugar, cinnamon, ginger, and salt. Add the melted butter and mix with a fork until small clumps form. Add the pecans and coconut. Mix gently to combine. Chill the crumb mixture while preparing the filling.

4. Preheat the oven to 375 degrees. In a small bowl, whisk together the brown sugar, cornstarch, nutmeg, cinnamon, crystallized ginger, and salt. Set aside.

5. Place the pineapple pieces between two pieces of paper towel. Press firmly to remove any excess liquid. In a large bowl, combine the pineapple pieces, sliced bananas, diced dried apricots, lemon juice, and rum, if using. Toss gently to mix. Sprinkle the sugar mixture over the fruit and toss to combine.

6. Remove the lined pie pan from the refrigerator or freezer. Transfer the fruit mixture into the lined pie pan. Top the pie evenly with the crumble mixture.

7. Place the pie on a baking sheet and bake in the preheated oven for 25 minutes. Reduce the temperature to 350 degrees and bake for an additional 15 minutes. If the crumb mixture begins browning too much, simply place a piece of foil loosely over the pie.

8. Remove the pie from the oven and let it cool on a wire rack at room temperature for at least 6 hours or overnight. Slice and serve with a nice scoop of vanilla ice cream and honey caramel sauce!

My obsession with honey began in Istanbul during a magical vacation. I discovered honeycomb, part of a traditional Turkish breakfast. On a subsequent trip to Rome, I encountered an incredible food shop that offered a dozen kinds of honey. Up until then, I thought the standard clover variety was all there was to honey. Wrong. Later on, a beekeeper near our farm inspired me to try my hand at beekeeping. Now, there's no shortage of honey at the farm. This pie combines local honey with buttermilk, cornmeal, and a touch of sea salt to make the perfect home-spun farm pie.

Salted Honey Chess Pie

Makes one 9-inch pie

Prep Time: 35 minutes

Baking Time: 16 minutes to blind bake the pie shell plus 40 to 45 minutes to bake the filled pie.

Crust

½ recipe Mary's Favorite Pie Dough, page 30

Filling

¾ cup honey

½ cup firmly packed light brown sugar

½ cup (4 ounces) unsalted butter, melted and slightly cooled

2 tablespoons all-purpose flour

2 tablespoons fine yellow cornmeal

1 tablespoon fresh lemon zest

¾ teaspoon salt

4 large eggs

½ cup buttermilk

1 teaspoon vanilla extract

Garnish

¾ cup chopped honey-roasted peanuts

Maldon sea salt flakes

Vanilla ice cream

Honey Caramel Sauce, page 223

1. Lightly dust your work surface with flour and roll the dough into an 11-inch round. Spray a 9-inch pie pan with nonstick cooking spray. Place the dough round in the prepared pan. Using kitchen scissors, trim the edge of the dough, leaving ¾-inch of overhang. Crimp or flute the side of the dough and refrigerate or freeze for 30 minutes.

2. Preheat the oven to 350 degrees. Remove the pastry-lined pie pan from the freezer or refrigerator. You will be partially baking the crust before filling the pie. Line the pan with parchment paper. Fill with pie weights or dried beans. Make sure the weights are evenly distributed around the pan bottom. Bake until the edge of the crust starts to brown, about 12 minutes. Remove from the oven and carefully lift the parchment paper (with the weights) out of the pan. Using a fork, make 6 light pricks in the bottom of the crust, being careful not to go all the way through. Return the pan to the oven and bake for 4 minutes. Remove from the oven and let it cool for 15 minutes before adding the filling. For more information on blind baking a crust, see page 29.

3. While the pie pastry is baking, prepare the filling. In a large mixing bowl, whisk together the honey, brown sugar, melted butter, flour, cornmeal, lemon zest, and salt. Add the eggs one at a time, whisking well after each addition. Add the buttermilk and vanilla and whisk to combine.

4. Place the pie on a baking sheet. Pour the filling into the pie pan. Loosely cover the edge of the crust with foil or a pie shield so it doesn't get overbaked. Bake until the filling is set, about 40 to 50 minutes. The center will jiggle slightly when shaken but should not be liquidy. Remove from the oven and cool completely on a wire rack for 2 to 3 hours. Garnish with the honey roasted peanuts and flaked sea salt. This pie is terrific served with a scoop of vanilla ice cream drizzled with my homemade honey caramel sauce.

Celebration Pies

I expect I'm not alone in saying I make the most pies during the holidays, particularly Thanksgiving. One year, a guest counted the number of pies I had made and announced there was one whole pie per person. Okay, I went overboard. But sometimes it is hard to narrow down selections when they are all so good.

And, since everyone has a favorite, I am not one to disappoint. Talk about going overboard, check out my mile-high pumpkin pie and my sweet potato pecan pie. They take the idea of holiday pie to a new level.

Finally, don't be afraid of my mincemeat pie. Although the name suggests otherwise, the pie contains no meat. Rather, the filling consists of fruit, spices and, of course, a little brandy.

All of the recipes in this chapter are truly ones to celebrate. To me, these pies are a blessing.

Some occasions simply call for pulling out all the stops. In this special treat—inspired by a version I tasted in Miami at Fireman Derek's Bake Shop—you get chocolate chip cookies, cheesecake, and pie all in one dessert. I say, why stop there? Add whipped cream, sugared pecans, and a drizzle of caramel and chocolate sauces. In my book, that makes this pie a real celebration!

Chocolate Chip Cheesecake Celebration Pie

Makes one 9-inch-deep dish pie

Prep Time: 65 minutes
Chilling Time: 6 hours or overnight

Chocolate Chip Cookie Crust

1¼ cup all-purpose flour
½ teaspoon baking soda
½ teaspoon salt
½ cup (4 ounces) unsalted butter, softened
⅓ cup granulated sugar
¼ cup firmly packed brown sugar
1 large egg
1½ teaspoon vanilla extract
1 cup bittersweet chocolate chips

Cheesecake Filling

12 ounces cream cheese, softened
½ cup sour cream
4 tablespoons (2 ounces) unsalted butter, softened
¾ cup granulated sugar
2 large eggs
½ teaspoon vanilla extract
¾ cup miniature chocolate chips

Sugared Pecans

2 teaspoons unsalted butter
3 ounces unsalted walnut or pecan pieces
2 tablespoons granulated sugar

Whipped Cream Topping

1½ cups heavy whipping cream, chilled
¼ cup confectioners' sugar
1 tablespoon cornstarch
2 tablespoons orange-flavored liqueur

Optional Toppings

Honey Caramel Sauce, page 223
Bittersweet Chocolate Sauce, page 221
Chocolate Curls, page 220

1. Spray a 9-inch-deep dish pie pan or 9-inch springform pan with nonstick cooking spray. Prepare the cookie crust. In a medium mixing bowl, sift together the flour, baking soda, and salt.

2. In the bowl of a stand mixer, beat the softened butter with both sugars until light and fluffy, about 2 minutes. With the mixer on medium, add the egg and vanilla. Beat until combined.

3. With the mixer on low, slowly add the dry ingredients until incorporated. Add the chocolate chips and mix briefly to combine.

4. Transfer the dough to the prepared pan. Using your hands, gently push the dough on the bottom and side of the pan. Refrigerate the lined pie pan for 30 minutes. While chilling, preheat the oven to 350 degrees.

5. Remove the pan from the refrigerator. Bake the pie crust for 18 to 20 minutes or until golden brown. Prepare the cheesecake filling while the crust is baking.

6. Using a stand mixer on medium speed, combine the cream cheese, sour cream, and butter. Mix until well blended, about 2 minutes. Reduce speed to medium low and add the sugar, eggs, and vanilla extract. Mix until just combined.

7. Sprinkle the miniature chocolate chips evenly over the baked cookie crust. Pour the cheesecake mixture over the chips. Cover the top of the pie with a 9-inch round of parchment paper. This will prevent the filling from becoming too brown. Bake for 30 minutes then remove the parchment paper. Bake an additional 15 minutes, for a total baking time of 45 minutes. Cool the pie on a rack. When completely cool, place in the refrigerator and chill 6 hours or overnight.

8. Now it's time to top the pie! Start by preparing the sugared nuts. Line a baking sheet with parchment paper. Melt the butter in a skillet over medium heat. When hot, add the nuts. Stir and toast in butter for 1 minute. Sprinkle with the sugar and toss to combine. Place the sugared pecans on the prepared pan in an even layer. Let cool. The nuts can be prepared a day ahead and stored in a ziplock bag after they are cooled.

9. When ready to serve the pie, prepare the whipped cream topping. Using a stand mixer with the whip attachment, beat the chilled cream on medium high until soft peaks form. Reduce the speed to medium and slowly add the confectioners' sugar, cornstarch, and the orange liqueur. Whip until firm peaks are formed. Using a large spatula, mound the whipped cream on top of the pie. Drizzle the pie with chocolate sauce and caramel sauce and sprinkle with the sugared pecans. Heck, why not put some chocolate curls on top too!

When you need to make just one holiday pie and can't decide between a pecan or a pumpkin pie, here is your answer. Make one pie into a two-fer. That's what makes this combination of sweet potato and pecans so special. You can enjoy the crunchy pecan topping and the creamy sweet potato filling all in one delicious hybrid of a pie. Who says you can't have it all?

Sweet Potato Pecan Pie

Makes one 9-inch pie

Prep Time: 1 hour and 30 minutes (includes time to make and chill pie pastry and cook the sweet potatoes)

Baking Time: 1 hour and 15 minutes

Crust

½ recipe Mary's Favorite Pie Dough, page 30

Sweet Potato Filling

1¼ cups packed cooked and mashed sweet potatoes (about 1 large or 2 medium roasted and peeled sweet potatoes)

1 tablespoon unsalted butter, melted and slightly cooled

2 teaspoons vanilla extract

⅓ cup firmly packed light brown sugar

¼ teaspoon ground cinnamon

⅛ teaspoon ground nutmeg

⅛ teaspoon ground cloves

¼ teaspoon salt

1 large egg yolk

1 tablespoon heavy cream

2 tablespoons granulated sugar

Pecan Filling

¾ cup granulated sugar

2 large eggs

1 tablespoon unsalted butter, melted and slightly cooled

¾ cup dark corn syrup

⅛ teaspoon ground cinnamon

Pinch of salt

1 teaspoon vanilla extract or 1 teaspoon bourbon

1 cup chopped or halved unsalted pecans

Garnish

1½ cups heavy whipping cream, chilled

3 tablespoons confectioners' sugar

1 tablespoon orange-flavored liqueur (optional)

1. Lightly dust your work surface with flour and roll the dough into an 11-inch round. Spray a 9-inch pie pan with nonstick cooking spray. Place the dough round in the prepared pan. Using kitchen scissors, trim the edge of the dough, leaving ¾-inch of overhang. Crimp or flute the side of the dough and refrigerate or freeze for 30 minutes.

2. While the pie shell pastry is chilling, preheat the oven to 325 degrees and make the 2 fillings. In a mixing bowl make the sweet potato filling by combining the mashed sweet potato, butter, vanilla extract, brown sugar, cinnamon, nutmeg, cloves, salt, egg yolk, heavy cream, and granulated sugar. Using a handheld mixer or stand mixer, beat on medium until smooth.

3. In another mixing bowl prepare the pecan filling. Combine the remaining ¾ cup granulated sugar, 2 eggs, melted butter, dark corn syrup, cinnamon, salt, and vanilla extract or bourbon. Whisk mixture until combined.

4. Remove the lined pie pan from the refrigerator or freezer. Place the pie pan on a baking sheet. Spread the sweet potato pie filling evenly in the pie shell. Now place the pecans evenly over the sweet potato filling. Using a rubber or silicone spatula, transfer the corn syrup mixture over the pecans, making sure to evenly cover the pecans.

5. Place the pie on a baking sheet and bake for 1 hour and 15 minutes. The pie should be firm on the top. If needed, bake for a few more minutes.

6. Remove the pie from the oven and let cool completely on a wire rack for at least 2 hours. When ready to serve, prepare the whipped cream. Place the cream in a chilled bowl of a stand mixer. Using the whip attachment, whip the cream on medium-high speed until soft peaks form. Reduce speed to medium and slowly add the confectioners' sugar and the orange liqueur, if using. Whip until firm peaks form. It's your choice how to use the whipped cream. You can pile it on top of the pie or slice the pie and top each serving with a mound of that delicious whipped cream!

It's simply not Thanksgiving without pumpkin pie. What gives this pumpkin pie extra pizazz is the airy, brown sugar meringue. I know—a topping of whipped cream is so delicious. BUT, when you taste how delicious the meringue is you will be glad you switched things up. The meringue is very stable and can be mounded and toasted several hours before serving. Right before I present the pie, I like to give the meringue a quick touch up with my kitchen torch for a little show before I serve it up to my waiting guests!

Mile-High Pumpkin Meringue Pie

Makes one 9-inch pie or tart

Prep Time: 1 hour
Cooking Time: 1 hour 20 minutes

Crust

½ recipe Mary's Favorite Pie Dough, page 30
or
Pâte Brisée, page 31

Filling

2 cups canned pumpkin

2 large eggs

⅓ cup granulated sugar

¼ cup firmly packed brown sugar

1 cup heavy whipping cream

½ teaspoon salt

½ teaspoon ground nutmeg

½ teaspoon ground cinnamon

1 teaspoon vanilla extract

Brown Sugar Meringue

¾ cup (6 large) egg whites, room temperature

1½ cups firmly packed brown sugar

⅓ cup water

¼ teaspoon cream of tartar

1. Lightly dust your work surface with flour and roll the dough into an 11-inch round. Spray a 9-inch tart pan with nonstick cooking spray. Place a 9-inch round of parchment paper on the bottom of the pan. Place the rolled-out dough into the prepared pan. Use a rolling pin to go over the top of the pan to trim off excess dough. Refrigerate or freeze the lined pan for 30 minutes while preparing the filling mixture.

2. Preheat the oven to 375 degrees. Place the pumpkin into the bowl of a food processor fitted with a steel blade. Add the eggs, both sugars, cream, salt, spices, and vanilla. Pulse to blend. Alternately, the ingredients can be placed in a large mixing bowl and combined using a wire whisk.

3. Remove the pan from the freezer or refrigerator and partially blind bake the crust. Line the chilled tart crust with parchment paper. Fill with pie weights or dried beans. Make sure the weights are evenly distributed around the pan bottom. Bake until the edges of the crust are starting to brown, about 12 minutes. Remove from the oven and carefully lift the parchment paper (with the weights) out of the pie tin. Using a fork, make 6 light pricks in the bottom of the crust, being careful not to go all the way through. Return tart crust to the oven and bake for 4 minutes. For more information on blind baking a crust, see page 29.

4. Place the partially blind-baked pastry-lined tart pan on a baking sheet. This makes transferring the tart to the oven easier. Transfer the pumpkin mixture into the pie shell. Bake until the filling is slightly puffed and firm to the touch, about 45 to 50 minutes. Cool on a rack until it reaches room temperature. The tart can be refrigerated for 2 to 3 days at this point. *(continued)*

Mile-High Pumpkin Meringue Pie

Continued

5. Prepare the meringue. When ready to finish the pie, preheat the oven to 325 degrees. Remove the top racks of the oven so there is plenty of room for the final baking of the meringue. Place the egg whites into the bowl of a stand mixer fitted with a whip attachment. Place the brown sugar and water in a small saucepot over medium heat. Heat mixture to the soft-ball stage (245 degrees). Use a candy thermometer to check the temperature. Do not stir the mixture, however you can "swirl" the pan now and then to remove any excess sugar buildup on the pan side.

6. While the sugar mixture is cooking, start whipping the egg whites on medium speed. When the whites are foamy, add the cream of tartar. Increase the speed to high and beat until the egg whites are fairly stiff. Turn the mixer to medium speed and slowly pour the hot sugar mixture into the whites. When all the sugar is added, increase the speed to medium high. Beat 5 to 6 minutes. The mixture should be very stiff but still slightly warm. You can tell when the meringue is done by placing your hands on the bottom of the bowl. If it is no longer hot, the meringue is cooled enough to use. If your meringue is ready before the sugar water reaches temp, just turn the mixer down to low so the whites get a little action. When ready to add the sugar mixture, just increase the speed to medium.

7. Place the pie on a baking sheet. This makes moving the pie to the oven easier. Using a large rubber spatula, spoon all of the meringue on top of the pie, forming a high dome. Use the back of a spoon to create peaks in the meringue. Make sure the meringue goes completely around the edge with no pumpkin pie exposed. Place the pie in the preheated oven and bake for 10 to 12 minutes. The meringue will set and turn a light brown.

8. Remove from the oven and let cool on a wire rack for 20 minutes or up to 2 hours. Use a small kitchen torch to get the meringue extra toasty just before serving.

My daughter Rebecca loves hazelnuts. I always have a jar of Nutella on hand for her to enjoy. She couldn't have been more delighted when I made this tart filled with bittersweet chocolate and a layer of delicious homemade hazelnut paste. It's one of her favorite desserts, and quickly became a favorite of the entire family.

Chocolate Ganache Hazelnut Tart

Makes one 9-inch round tart or one 14 by 4.5-inch rectangular tart

Prep Time: 35 minutes
Baking Time: 10 minutes
Cooling Time: 6 hours

Crust

½ cup (about 2 ounces) toasted hazelnuts (see note)

8 whole graham crackers, broken into pieces (about 2 cups of crumbs)

2 tablespoons dark brown sugar

4 tablespoons (2 ounces) unsalted butter, melted and slightly cooled

1 tablespoon Frangelico™ (hazelnut liqueur), optional

Filling

12 ounces coarsely chopped bittersweet chocolate

⅓ cup hazelnut paste (see note)

1½ cups heavy cream

1 tablespoon Frangelico™ (hazelnut liqueur), optional

Garnish

¾ cup coarsely chopped toasted hazelnuts

1. Line a tart pan with a removable bottom with parchment paper. Spray the pan bottom and sides with nonstick cooking spray. Set aside while preparing the crust.

2. If you have not done so, toast and skin your hazelnuts (directions are below). Preheat the oven to 350 degrees. In the bowl of a food processor, combine the hazelnuts, graham crackers, and brown sugar. Pulse to form a fine crumb mixture. With the processor on, drizzle the butter through the feed tube along with the liqueur, if using. Transfer the mixture to the prepared tart pan and, using your fingers, press the crumbs firmly into the bottom and sides of the pan. Refrigerate or freeze the lined tart pan for 30 minutes then place on a baking sheet and bake for 10 minutes. Cool on a rack before filling the tart.

3. Place the chopped chocolate and hazelnut paste into a heat-proof mixing bowl. In a small pot, heat the heavy cream until small bubbles appear on the side. Pour the hot cream over the chocolate and hazelnut paste. Let sit for 1 minute then stir until completely smooth. If using, stir in the hazelnut liqueur.

4. Using a large plastic spatula, transfer the chocolate mixture into the crust. Using an offset spatula, smooth the top of the mixture. Refrigerate for 6 hours or overnight.

5. When ready to serve, decorate the top of the tart with the remaining coarsely chopped toasted hazelnuts. *Tip:* When you are ready to cut the tart into serving pieces, warm the blade of your knife under hot water then wipe dry with a kitchen towel. The slight warmth on the knife blade will make it glide right through that firm chocolate filling.

How To Toast Hazelnuts

Preheat the oven to 350 degrees. Place whole skin-on hazelnuts on a parchment-lined baking sheet. Toast in the oven until lightly browned, about 10 to 14 minutes. Remove the pan and transfer the nuts to a clean kitchen towel. Wrap the towel around the nuts and gently rub with your hands in a back-and-forth motion. You are trying to remove the hazelnut skins. Open up the towel and transfer the nuts only (leaving the skin on the towel) to a bowl. You will probably have a small bit of skin that remains on the hazelnuts. That is okay. If your hazelnuts come without the skin, you will still need to toast them, but you will not need to rub them in the towel to remove the skins.

Hazelnut Paste

Makes approximately ¾ cup

2 cups toasted and skinned hazelnuts
1 teaspoon grapeseed oil
A high-speed blender

Place the hazelnuts in a high-speed blender and process until they are very fine. Using a spatula, move all the hazelnuts down to the bottom of the blender. Add the grapeseed oil. Continue pulsing, pushing down the hazelnut mixture now and then, until the mixture is creamy like smooth peanut butter. This may take a while, but suddenly, a creamy hazelnut spread will appear! Store the hazelnut paste in a clean container at room temperature in your pantry like you would store peanut butter.

This version of my mom's recipe has lots of fresh and dried fruit, brandy or cognac, and alluring spices. The name comes from a 500-year-old means of preserving meat with suet. As a child, I couldn't fathom a sweet pie with "meat" in the name. Later I learned the pie had no meat at all! Whether you grew up with mincemeat pie or are new to the party, I think you'll enjoy this traditional close to a holiday dinner. *Tip:* Prepare the filling a week to 10 days in advance and rest it in the fridge to meld the flavors.

Mincemeat Pie

Makes one 9-inch double-crust or lattice pie

Prep Time: 35 minutes plus 1 week for the mincemeat to rest in the fridge
Baking Time: 55 to 60 minutes

Filling
1 large orange, zested, peeled, and diced
2 large apples, peeled, cored, and diced
1 cup golden raisins
½ cup chopped dried apricots
½ cup dried cherries or dried cranberries
⅓ cup firmly packed brown sugar
½ teaspoon lemon juice
½ teaspoon ground cinnamon
½ teaspoon ground cloves
¼ teaspoon ground nutmeg
¼ teaspoon salt
½ cup brandy or cognac
½ cup water

Crust
Mary's Favorite Pie Dough, page 30

Egg Wash
1 large egg
1 tablespoon heavy cream

1. Make the filling 1 week before you are going to prepare the pie. Zest and peel the orange. Discard the orange peel but keep the zest. Dice the orange pieces.

2. In a large saucepan, combine all of the filling ingredients, including the orange zest and orange pieces. Cook over low heat, covered, for about 40 minutes. Stir the mixture periodically. The dried fruit should become plump as the liquid thickens.

3. Using an immersion blender or food processor, pulse the mixture until it becomes a rough puree. Be careful not to over-process. There should still be some roughness to the mixture. Cool to room temperature and store in the refrigerator for at least 1 week and up to 2 weeks for the flavors to deepen.

4. When ready to prepare the pie, preheat the oven to 375 degrees. Remove 1 dough disk from the refrigerator 30 minutes before you are ready to roll it out. Lightly dust your work surface with flour and roll the dough into an 11-inch round. Spray a 9-inch pie pan with nonstick cooking spray. Place the dough round in the prepared pan. Using kitchen scissors, trim the edge of the dough, leaving ¾-inch of overhang.

5. Transfer the filling mixture into the lined pie pan. In a small bowl, whisk together the egg and cream. Set the egg wash to the side.

6. On a lightly floured work surface, roll out the remaining dough disk into an 11-inch round. If making a double-crust pie, lightly brush the dough side with egg wash. Transfer the round of pastry to the top of the pie and press lightly on the edge to adhere the 2 pieces. Trim the dough side to ¾-inch. Crimp or flute the pie edge using your fingers or a fork. Using a paring knife, cut 3 slits on the top of the pie to release steam during baking. Alternatively, you can top the pie with a lattice crust or decorate with pastry cutouts. See page 28 for instructions on how to make a lattice top. Brush the top pie crust or cutouts with the egg wash.

7. Place the pie on a baking sheet. Bake on the middle rack of the oven for 55 to 60 minutes or until the top crust is golden brown. Remove from the oven and transfer to a wire rack. Cool completely to set, about 3 to 4 hours.

Cranberries aren't just for Thanksgiving and pies aren't just for dessert! I love to tuck cranberries into this versatile savory tart that makes for a great appetizer or entree. Depending on your preference, the tart can be made into a round, rectangle, or square. In any shape, it's perfect for holiday entertaining.

Walnut, Blue Cheese, and Cranberry Tart

Makes one quarter-size sheet (9 by 13-inch baking sheet)

Prep Time: 40 minutes

Baking Time: 40 minutes

Crust

1⅓ cups all-purpose flour plus 2 tablespoons, divided

⅔ cup ground walnuts

1 tablespoon sugar

¼ teaspoon salt

½ teaspoon dry mustard

A pinch of cayenne pepper

7 tablespoons unsalted butter, chilled and diced into ½-inch cubes

1 tablespoon plus 1 teaspoon half and half

Filling

1 tablespoon olive oil

1¼ cups diced white onion

½ teaspoon salt

1 tablespoon sugar

2 cups finely chopped walnuts

1½ cups whole cranberries, fresh or frozen

1 tablespoon chopped fresh thyme leaves

3 large eggs

1½ cups heavy cream

5 ounces crumbled blue cheese

1. Spray nonstick cooking spray on the bottom and sides of the baking sheet. Line the bottom of the sheet with parchment paper.

2. In a food processor, make the pastry dough by combining 1⅓ cups flour, walnuts, sugar, salt, mustard, and cayenne. Pulse to combine. With the processor on, add the butter cubes, one at a time, through the feed tube. Add the half and half. The dough should come together when pinched with your fingers.

3. Place the remaining 2 tablespoons of flour in a small bowl. Dip your fingertips into the flour and press the dough evenly on the bottom and sides of the sheet. Refrigerate or freeze the dough-lined sheet for 30 minutes or up to 2 weeks.

4. Preheat the oven to 375 degrees. Remove the lined pie sheet from the refrigerator or freezer. You will be partially baking the crust before filling the tart. Line the tart sheet with parchment paper. Fill with pie weights or dried beans. Make sure the weights are evenly distributed around the sheet bottom. Bake until the edges of the crust start to brown, about 16 minutes. Remove from the oven and carefully lift out the parchment paper and pie weights. For more information on blind baking a tart or pie, see page 29.

5. Now it's time to make the delicious filling! Heat the olive oil in a skillet over medium heat. Add the onions and sprinkle with salt. Sauté until translucent, about 2 minutes. Sprinkle with the sugar and cook on medium heat, stirring occasionally, until lightly caramelized, about 3 more minutes. Turn off heat. Add the walnuts, cranberries, and thyme.

6. In a bowl, whisk together the eggs and cream. Transfer the walnut-cranberry mixture into the tart crust. Spread the filling evenly to cover the entire sheet. Crumble blue cheese over the top of the tart. Pour the egg mixture evenly over the filling.

7. Bake in a 375 degree oven until set, about 22 to 25 minutes. Remove from the oven and place the sheet on a cooling rack for 15 minutes. Cut into squares and serve warm or at room temperature.

Pistachios are one of my favorite nuts. When I was in college, my mom regularly sent bags of them for snacking. Now, I like to finish the ends of cannoli with oodles of pistachios and always add them to my biscotti dough. In this tart, I tuck the little gems wherever I can – in the crust, in the filling, and sprinkled on top for good measure. The only thing that makes this tart better is – you guessed it – a big scoop of vanilla ice cream.

Bittersweet Chocolate Pistachio Tart

Makes one 9-inch tart

Prep Time: 1 hour and 15 minutes
Baking Time: 22 to 24 minutes
(for crust only)

Chocolate Crust

½ cup (4 ounces) unsalted butter, softened

¼ cup granulated sugar

¾ teaspoon vanilla extract

¾ cup all-purpose flour

¼ cup unsweetened cocoa powder

⅓ cup unsalted finely chopped shelled pistachios (measure chopped not whole pistachios)

¼ teaspoon salt

Pistachio Paste

1 cup unsalted chopped shelled pistachios (measure chopped not whole pistachios)

½ cup granulated sugar

¼ teaspoon salt

2 tablespoons plus 2 teaspoons neutral oil like grapeseed or safflower oil

Filling

12 ounces coarsely chopped bittersweet chocolate

1½ cups heavy cream

Garnish

½ cup finely chopped unsalted pistachios

1. Place the softened butter in the bowl of a stand mixer fitted with the paddle attachment. Beat on medium until lightened then slowly add the sugar and vanilla. Beat on medium for 3 minutes.

2. In a mixing bowl, combine the flour, cocoa powder, pistachios, and salt. With the mixer on low, slowly add the flour mixture to the butter mixture, and beat until combined. Remove dough from the mixer and form it into a ball. Using the palm of your hand, press down to form a disk. Wrap the dough in plastic wrap and refrigerate for 30 minutes.

3. Spray the bottom and side of a 9-inch tart pan with a removable bottom with nonstick cooking spray. Line the bottom of the pan with a round of parchment paper. On a lightly floured work surface, roll the chilled dough into a 12-inch circle. Transfer the dough to the prepared pan, gently pressing it into the pan bottom and side. Use a rolling pin or sharp knife to trim the dough flush with the pan side. Refrigerate or freeze the dough-lined pan for 30 minutes. Preheat the oven to 325 degrees.

4. Remove the pan from the freezer or refrigerator. We will be blind baking the crust completely before filling the tart. Line the chilled pastry-lined tart pan with parchment paper. Fill with pie weights or dried beans. Make sure the weights are evenly distributed around the pan bottom. Bake for 14 minutes. Remove tart from the oven and carefully lift the parchment paper (with the weights) out of the tart. Using a fork, make 6 light pricks in the bottom of the crust, being careful not to go all the way through. Return tart crust to the oven and bake for 8 to 10 minutes or until the bottom of the crust is firm. Remove from the oven and let cool for 15 minutes before filling the tart. For more information on blind baking a crust, see page 29.

5. In the bowl of a food processor, combine 1 cup chopped pistachios, sugar, and salt. Pulse until the mixture is incorporated. Add the oil and pulse until the mixture forms a paste. Transfer the pistachio paste to the crust. Use a small offset spatula to smooth out the paste into an even layer. Place in the refrigerator while preparing the chocolate filling. This will chill the pistachio paste so it does not "bleed" into the chocolate layer.

6. Place the chocolate in a heat-proof bowl. In a saucepan, heat the cream until bubbles form on the side of the pan. Pour the cream over the chopped chocolate. Let stand for several minutes then use a spatula to mix to a smooth consistency.

7. Remove the chilled tart crust from the refrigerator. Pour the chocolate mixture over the pistachio mixture. Using an offset spatula, smooth out the chocolate filling.

8. Refrigerate for 3 to 4 hours or overnight. When ready to serve, remove the tart pan side and place the tart on a serving platter. Garnish with the remaining ½ cup pistachios.

I first tried frangipane at one of my favorite Italian cafes. I fell in love immediately. Frangipane, with its velvety almond cream enhanced with a hint of vanilla, is pure heaven. I created this delicious tart with my favorite kind of jam, raspberry. It's the perfect marriage. This tart is not only delicious, it's a show-stopper, especially with the elegant fluted crust and fresh raspberries on top.

Fresh Raspberry and Frangipane Tart

Makes one 9-inch tart

Prep Time: 1 hour
Baking Time: 55 total minutes
(includes 20 minutes for the blind bake and 40 minutes additional to finish the tart)

Raspberry Jam

2 cups raspberries, fresh or frozen
½ cup granulated sugar
1 teaspoon fresh lemon juice

Sweet Almond Pastry Crust

¾ cup almond flour
½ cup all-purpose flour
½ cup confectioners' sugar
A pinch of salt
6 tablespoons (3 ounces) unsalted butter, chilled and cut into small cubes
1 large egg yolk
½ teaspoon vanilla extract

Frangipane Filling

1¼ cups almond flour
2 tablespoons all-purpose flour
½ cup granulated sugar
½ cup (4 ounces) unsalted butter, softened
1 large egg
1 large egg white
1 teaspoon vanilla extract
¼ teaspoon salt

Garnish

2 cups fresh raspberries
Confectioners' sugar for dusting the final tart

1. In a saucepan, combine all the jam ingredients. Heat on medium low and simmer for 25 to 30 minutes, stirring frequently, until the jam is thickened. Remove from the heat and transfer into a bowl. Let cool at room temperature. The jam can be used in about 2 hours or covered with plastic wrap and refrigerated for up to 1 week.

2. To prepare the crust, place the almond flour, all-purpose flour, confectioners' sugar, and salt in the bowl of a food processor. With the processor running, add the butter, a little at a time, through the feed tube. With the processor on, add the egg yolk and vanilla through the feed tube. The dough will be rather soft but should come together when pinched between your fingers.

3. Spray a 9-inch tart pan with a removable bottom with nonstick pan spray. Place a 9-inch round of parchment paper on the bottom of the pan. Transfer the pastry dough to the pan. If the dough is too sticky to roll out, lightly flour your fingertips and press the dough evenly into the bottom and up the side of the pan. Using a fork, make 6 light pricks in the bottom of the crust, being careful not to go all the way through. Refrigerate or freeze for 30 minutes or overnight.

4. Prepare the frangipane while the crust is chilling. In the clean bowl of your food processor, combine all the frangipane ingredients. Process until the filling is smooth and a creamy consistency. Set the filling aside.

5. Preheat the oven to 350 degrees. Remove the pan from the refrigerator or freezer. We will be doing a partial blind bake on the crust. Line the tart pan with parchment paper. Fill with pie weights or dried beans. Make sure the weights are evenly distributed around the pan bottom. Bake until the edges of the crust are starting to brown, about 12 minutes. Remove from the oven and carefully lift the parchment paper (with the weights) out of the tart pan. Using a fork, make 6 light pricks in the bottom of the crust, being careful not to go all the way through. Return to the oven and bake for 8 minutes or until the bottom of the crust begins to brown. Remove from the oven and let cool on a rack for 15 minutes before filling the tart. For more information on blind baking a crust, see page 29. *(continued)*

Fresh Raspberry and Frangipane Tart

Continued

6. When ready to bake, spread the cooled raspberry jam evenly on the bottom of the partially blind-baked tart crust. Spoon the frangipane over the jam. Use an offset spatula to spread the almond cream to the edge of the tart.

7. Place the tart on a baking sheet and bake on the middle rack of the preheated oven for 35 to 40 minutes or until the top is a light golden-brown color and a toothpick inserted in the middle comes out clean. Allow the tart to cool completely on a rack then remove the outer tart ring and place on a serving platter.

8. Place the raspberries in the center of the tart in a concentric circle, filling up the entire tart top. Dust tart with confectioners' sugar.

Eggnog is surely one of the tastiest treats during the holiday season. If you like eggnog, it's time to try it in the form of a pie. And, in this case, little-bitty mini pies! This recipe is creamy and a little boozy. I promise you, no one will say they don't have room for dessert! George Washington is said to have devised his own secret recipe for eggnog, and that only the hardiest of guests would partake in the concoction. If it's good enough for George, it's good enough for me—and pie. Here's to good health and prosperity in the new year!

Eggnog Pie Bites

Makes approximately 40 pie bites

Prep Time: 45 minutes plus 30 minutes to chill unbaked crust

Baking Time: 18 to 22 minutes

Chilling Time: Overnight

Pie Pastry

Pâte Brisée, page 31

Filling

1½ teaspoons unflavored gelatin

2 tablespoons cold water

3 tablespoons granulated sugar

1 tablespoon cornstarch

⅛ teaspoon salt

1 cup eggnog

½ teaspoon vanilla extract

1 teaspoon rum

⅛ teaspoon ground nutmeg

½ cup heavy cream

Rum Nutmeg Whipped Cream Garnish

¾ cup heavy cream, chilled

2 tablespoons confectioners' sugar

½ teaspoon rum

A pinch of ground nutmeg

1. Spray mini-muffin tin wells with nonstick cooking spray. Shape the chilled dough into 40 balls approximately 1-inch in diameter. Press each ball into the muffin pan wells, spreading the dough evenly on the bottom and side of each well. You can use a mini-tart tamper tool for this if you have one. If using this tool, dip it in flour, then press each ball in the well with even pressure. The dough will rise slightly above the rim of the well. Refrigerate or freeze for 30 minutes.

2. Preheat the oven to 350 degrees. Remove the pan from the refrigerator or freezer and blind bake the pastry. We will be baking the mini-tart shells completely before filling them. Bake for approximately 18 to 22 minutes or until the pastry is light brown. For more information on blind baking a crust, see page 29.

3. In a small bowl, sprinkle the gelatin over the cold water. Let stand for 1 minute.

4. In a saucepan, whisk together the sugar, cornstarch, and salt. Add the eggnog and whisk until smooth. Set the pan on medium heat and bring to a bowl, whisking constantly. The mixture should begin to thicken in about 2 minutes. Stir in the gelatin and whisk until dissolved. Remove from the heat. Stir in the vanilla extract, rum, and nutmeg. Let the mixture cool completely at room temperature before folding in the whipped cream.

5. In a chilled bowl using a handheld mixer, beat the ½ cup heavy cream until medium peaks are formed. Gently fold the whipped cream into the cooled eggnog mixture. Transfer the filling into the baked and cooled mini-tart shells. I like to use a pastry bag to pipe the filling into the baked shells. Refrigerate until the filling is firm, preferably overnight.

6. When ready to serve, prepare the rum nutmeg whipped cream. Place the cream in a chilled bowl of a stand mixer. Using the whip attachment, whip the cream on medium-high speed until soft peaks form. Reduce speed to medium and slowly add the confectioners' sugar followed by the rum and nutmeg. Whip until firm peaks form. Use a teaspoon to top each mini tart with the whipped cream. You can also use a pastry bag to pipe a small swirl of whipped cream on top of each mini pie bite.

In Italy, Christmas Eve is often referred to as La Vigilia, or vigil. The Feast of the Seven Fishes Pie has special roots in Southern Italy where it is served on this special holiday.

Mild white-fleshed fish like whitefish, cod, or sole work well in this dish. I add shellfish, favoring a combination of shrimp and scallops. You can also elevate this dish with lobster. And if you really want to send this pie over the top, serve it with crème fraîche and caviar. Time to celebrate!

Feast of the Seven Fishes Pie

Makes a 1½-quart casserole serving 6 to 8

Prep Time: 50 minutes

Baking Time: 35 to 40 minutes

Filling

1 pound mild fish filets, cut into 1-inch chunks

½ pound peeled and deveined shrimp

½ pound large sea scallops, rinsed and patted dry

1 cup diced lobster meat (optional)

7 tablespoons unsalted butter, divided

1½ cups halved and thinly sliced leeks (about 1 large or 2 medium)

2 carrots, peeled and cut into a ¼-inch dice

2 garlic cloves, minced

⅓ cup all-purpose flour

½ cup vermouth or white wine

1¼ cups whole milk

1 cup heavy cream

1 cup frozen peas, thawed

2 teaspoons drained and rinsed capers

¼ teaspoon salt

¼ teaspoon ground white pepper

2 tablespoons fresh chopped tarragon
or
2 teaspoons dried tarragon

2 tablespoons chopped fresh Italian parsley

Egg Wash

1 large egg

1 tablespoon cream

Top Crust

1 to 2 sheets frozen puff pastry, thawed

Optional Garnish

Crème fraîche, store bought or homemade, page 223

Salmon, whitefish, or trout caviar

1. Line a baking sheet with a paper towel. Place all the fish and shellfish evenly spaced on the paper towel. Place another paper towel over the fish and shellfish. Press firmly on the paper towel. Remove the top towel and place another paper towel on top. Press firmly again so that as much liquid is removed from the fish/seafood as possible. Place in the refrigerator on the paper towel-lined pan until ready to use.

2. Butter a 1½ quart casserole dish with 1 tablespoon of the butter. Set aside.

3. Place the sliced leeks in a colander and wash under cool water. Dry the leeks with a paper towel.

4. In a large skillet, melt the remaining 6 tablespoons of butter over medium heat. Add the leeks and cook until soft, stirring frequently. Add the carrots and cook for 2 more minutes. Add the garlic and cook for 30 seconds.

5. Sprinkle the flour over the vegetable mixture and stir to coat. Cook for 1 minute on medium heat, stirring constantly, to cook the flour. Deglaze the pan with the vermouth or white wine and stir to combine. Add the milk and cream. Simmer on medium heat, stirring frequently, until the mixture thickens, about 3 to 4 minutes. Add the peas, capers, salt, white pepper, tarragon, and Italian parsley. Mix gently to combine. You can taste the mixture at this point for seasoning. One note of caution: the capers will have a salty flavor so be careful not to oversalt the mixture.

6. Transfer to a large mixing bowl and let cool to room temperature. After you add the fish you will not be able to taste the mixture, so make sure to check seasoning at this point. This mixture, without the fish and shellfish, can be prepared 1 day ahead. Cover the cooled mixture with plastic wrap and refrigerate until ready to use.

7. Preheat the oven to 425 degrees. Add the fish and shellfish and stir gently to combine. Transfer the mixture to the prepared casserole dish. *(continued)*

Feast of the Seven Fishes Pie

Continued

8. In a small mixing bowl, combine the egg with the cream. Lightly flour your work surface and unroll 1 piece of puff pastry. Using a rolling pin, roll the pastry to a ⅛-inch thickness. Using a paring knife, cut the dough ½-inch larger than the top of your casserole dish. Place the pastry on top of the filled casserole, pushing the side pastry into the casserole to form a side crust. Brush the pastry with the egg wash.

9. Now it's time to get creative! Use the remaining piece of puff pastry to decorate the top of your casserole. You can make circles from the pastry and add them to the top like scales, or you can use a fish-shaped cookie cutter to make fish shapes to go on top. Remember to brush the top of any decorations with the egg wash so they get nicely browned during baking. Finally, cut a few ½-inch slits in the crust to let steam escape during baking.

10. Place the casserole dish on a baking sheet and bake until the pastry is golden brown, about 35 to 40 minutes. Remove from the oven and let cool on a rack for 10 minutes before serving. If using, serve with the crème fraîche and caviar. Time to celebrate!

I have had a love affair with brownies since I was a little girl and made batches after school to share with neighbors. While exploring Miami, I discovered the most delicious, perfectly fudgy, brownie pie. That pie inspired me to create these chocolatey pie bars. What I love about my recipe is the addition of espresso powder to bring out an intense chocolate flavor. I didn't stop there *(of course!)*. I added espresso powder to the chocolate whipped cream. If you want to get super fancy, add some chocolate curls with a drizzle of chocolate sauce on top, or add a handful of mini chocolate chips.

Chocolate Brownie Pie Bars

Makes one 9-inch square pan

Prep Time: 35 minutes

Baking Time: 16 minutes to blind bake crust plus 25 to 30 minutes to bake the filling

Crust

½ recipe Mary's Favorite Pie Dough, page 30

or

½ recipe Pâte Brisée, page 31

Filling

½ cup (4 ounces) unsalted butter, melted and cooled

1 tablespoon vegetable oil

½ cup granulated sugar

½ cup firmly packed brown sugar

2 large eggs, room temperature

1½ teaspoons vanilla extract

½ cup all-purpose flour

A pinch of salt

½ cup cocoa powder

½ teaspoon espresso powder, optional

¾ cup bittersweet chocolate chips

½ cup chopped walnuts, optional

Chocolate Espresso Whipped Cream Garnish

1½ cups heavy cream, chilled

3 tablespoons confectioners' sugar

2 tablespoons plus 1 teaspoon cocoa powder

1 teaspoon vanilla extract

A pinch of fine sea salt

½ teaspoon espresso powder, optional

Garnish

Bittersweet chocolate curls, page 220

1. Spray a 9-inch square pan with nonstick cooking spray. Roll out the dough into a 12-inch square about ⅛-inch thick. Transfer dough to the prepared pie pan. Using your fingertips, gently press the dough up the sides of the pan. Trim off the excess dough and crimp or flute the pastry edge. Refrigerate or freeze the lined pie pan for 30 minutes. Chilling the dough will make the dough firm so it doesn't shrink during baking.

2. Preheat the oven to 350 degrees. Remove the lined pan from the refrigerator or freezer. You will be partially baking the crust before filling the pie. Line the pan with parchment paper. Fill with pie weights or dried beans. Make sure the weights are evenly distributed around the pan bottom. Bake until the edges of the crust start to brown, about 12 minutes. Remove from the oven and carefully lift out the parchment paper (with the weights). Using a fork, make 6 light pricks in the bottom of the crust, being careful not to go all the way through. Return pie crust to the oven and bake for 4 minutes. Remove from the oven and let cool for 15 minutes before adding the filling. For more information on blind baking a crust, see page 29.

3. When crust is cool, begin making the filling. In a mixing bowl, combine the melted and cooled butter with the oil, granulated sugar, and brown sugar. Add the eggs, one at a time, whisking after each addition. Add the vanilla extract and mix to combine.

4. In a mixing bowl, sift together the flour, salt, cocoa powder, and espresso powder, if using. Gently fold the dry ingredients into the wet ingredients. Fold in the bittersweet chocolate chips and the walnuts, if using.

5. Transfer the filling into the crust and bake in the preheated oven for approximately 25 to 30 minutes or until a toothpick inserted in the center of the pie comes out clean. Remove from the oven and let cool on a rack for approximately 1 hour before slicing.

6. When ready to serve, prepare the whipped cream. Place the cream in a chilled bowl of a stand mixer. Using the whip attachment, whip the cream on medium-high speed until soft peaks form. Reduce speed to medium and slowly add the confectioners' sugar, cocoa powder, vanilla extract, sea salt, and espresso powder if using. Whip until firm peaks form. Cut the brownie pie into squares and place on serving plates. Mound the whipped cream on top of the cooled brownie bars. Garnish the top of the pie bars with chocolate curls.

Fruit Pies

My mother always loved a classic fruit pie. Who doesn't? She also taught me that the key to good pie baking was to always use what was in season. So off we would go to the local orchard to pick whatever fruit was in season right from the tree.

I still love a classic blueberry pie or my peachy peach pie, but sometimes I like to make a real showstopper like my fancy apple rose tart or fig mascarpone tart.

This chapter has it all when it comes to fruit. From classic pies to fancy tarts, these recipes won't disappoint. Give a little love to your local orchard or farmers market and pick up that fresh fruit. Believe me, you'll taste the difference.

This tart is almost too beautiful to eat. You must, however, because it is absolutely delicious. I use Pink Lady apples so the tips of the apple roses have a slight red tint. Slice carefully (a mandoline is a must), then roll the slices into delicate, edible "roses" and place on top of my pâte sucrée crust. For a tart with a "wow" factor, this is it!

Apple Rose Tart

Makes one 9-inch tart

Prep Time: 1 hour
Baking Time: 34 minutes

Crust
½ recipe Pâte Sucrée, page 32

Filling
3 tablespoons unsalted butter, melted
¼ cup granulated sugar
1 teaspoon vanilla extract
½ teaspoon ground cinnamon

Apple Roses
4 to 5 large Pink Lady apples
Juice of 1 lemon
3 tablespoons unsalted butter
¼ cup granulated sugar

Glaze
½ cup apricot preserves
1 tablespoon orange-flavored liqueur

1. Lightly spray a 9-inch tart pan with a removable bottom with nonstick cooking spray. Line the bottom of the pan with a round of parchment paper. Lightly flour your work surface and roll the dough out into a 12-inch circle. Drape the dough gently in the pan. Using your fingers, press the dough on the bottom and side of the pan. Use a rolling pin or sharp knife to trim the dough flush with the pan side. Refrigerate or freeze the dough-lined pan for 30 minutes.

2. Preheat the oven to 350 degrees. Remove the pan from the refrigerator or freezer and blind bake the crust. You will be baking the crust completely before filling the tart as the apples take only a few minutes to bake once they are placed in the tart. Line the chilled tart pastry with parchment paper. Fill with pie weights or dried beans. Make sure the weights are evenly distributed around the pan bottom. Bake until the edges of the crust are starting to brown, about 15 to 16 minutes. Remove the tart pan from the oven and carefully lift the parchment paper (with the weights) out of the pan. Using a fork, make 6 light pricks in the bottom of the crust, being careful not to go all the way through. Return to the oven and bake for 8 minutes or until the bottom is light brown. Remove from the oven and let cool for 15 minutes before filling the tart. For more information on blind baking a crust, see page 29.

3. While the tart crust is in the oven, prepare the filling. In a small bowl whisk together 3 tablespoons melted butter, sugar, vanilla, and cinnamon. Set aside.

4. Prepare the apple roses. Cut the apples in quarters and use a paring knife to remove any of the stem and seeds. Do not use an apple corer. You want to be able to slice nice "half-moon" pieces of apple. In a heat-proof mixing bowl, combine the lemon juice, remaining 3 tablespoons melted butter, and the ¼ cup sugar. Mix to combine. *(continued)*

Apple Rose Tart

Continued

5. Using a mandoline slicer, carefully slice the apple quarters into very thin half-moon slices. Place the apple slices in the bowl with the lemon butter mixture and toss gently to coat. Place a piece of plastic wrap loosely on top of the bowl and begin microwaving the apples in 30-second intervals, tossing the apples gently between each spurt. The goal is to evenly soften the apples. Continue for two more 30-second spurts. Test an apple slice to see if it is pliable. The apples are ready when you can easily take an apple slice and roll it tightly into a cylinder. If the apples are still a bit hard, simply process them for another 30 seconds.

6. If the tart crust is still baking and cooling, you can still begin making apple roses. Start by rolling a piece of apple into a tight cylinder. This will be the rose center. Now take individual slices and start adhering them to the center piece to create petals. You can make the roses different sizes if you like or have them be more uniform in size. It's all up to you. This is where you can really get creative!

7. Transfer the filling mixture into the cooled baked tart shell. Using a small offset spatula, evenly cover the tart bottom. Now start filling the tart with the apple roses, making them very compact. You will need to fill the entire tart with roses!

8. Once the apple roses are in the tart, it is time for the final bake. Bake the tart in the 350-degree oven for 10 minutes. While the tart is baking, prepare the glaze. In a small saucepan, melt the apricot preserves with the orange liqueur. Place the melted preserves in a small mesh strainer that has been placed over a small bowl. Using the back of a spoon, press the apricot mixture through the sieve.

9. Remove the baked tart from the oven and place on a cooling rack. While the tart is still warm, use a pastry brush to lightly brush the top of the roses with the glaze. Let the tart cool for 30 minutes before removing the pan side.

Bumbleberry is my absolute favorite berry pie. Now, you may wonder what exactly is a bumbleberry? The answer is: it doesn't exist! Bumbleberry refers to the "bumble" of berries that make up this delicious pie filling mixture. My recipe editor, Terri, adds deliciously sour Montmorency cherries from Door County, Wisconsin to the mix. Since cherries have a limited season, I load up on fresh cherries when they are available and freeze the pitted fruit in storage bags. When I have a craving for bumbleberry pie, all I need to do is go to my frozen stash of cherries and add them to the berry mix!

Bumbleberry Individual Galettes

10 individual galettes

Prep Time: 45 minutes
Baking Time: 30 minutes

Crust
Mary's Favorite Pie Dough, page 30

Filling
2 cups pitted fresh sour cherries
2 cups fresh blueberries
2 cups fresh raspberries or blackberries
2 teaspoons fresh lemon juice
1 cup granulated sugar
⅓ cup all-purpose flour
1 tablespoon tapioca

Egg Glaze
1 large egg
1 tablespoon cream

Garnish
Demerara or raw sugar

1. Lightly dust your work surface with flour. Divide dough into 10 pieces. Roll each dough piece into a 6 to 7-inch round.

2. Preheat the oven to 425 degrees. In a large mixing bowl, combine the cherries, berries, lemon juice, and sugar. Toss gently to combine. Add the flour and tapioca, tossing gently to coat the berries.

3. Divide the filling evenly among the 10 dough rounds, keeping a ¾-inch area around the circumference free of filling. Using your finger, bring up the dough edge to come slightly over the filling and pinch to create "pleats" in the dough.

4. Combine the egg with the cream. Lightly brush the galette dough edge with the egg wash. Sprinkle lightly with the raw sugar.

5. Place the galettes on a baking sheet. Bake in the preheated oven for 10 minutes. Reduce the heat to 350 degrees and continue baking until the galettes are golden brown, about another 20 minutes. Remove from the oven and let cool on a rack for 2 hours before serving.

I discovered guava as a student in Argentina at the local markets and rekindled my love for the fruit as a snowbird in Miami. Guava has a unique taste—a cross between a strawberry and a pear. It has a pronounced tropical flair, and I always look forward to enjoying this pie when going south for the winter.

Guava Berry Ginger Pie

Makes one 9-inch lattice topped pie

Prep Time: 35 minutes
Baking Time: 45 minutes

Crust
Mary's Favorite Pie Dough, page 30
or
Pâte Brisée, page 31

Filling
1 cup granulated sugar
1 teaspoon lemon zest
4 tablespoons cornstarch
2 teaspoons very finely grated, peeled fresh ginger or 1 tablespoon candied ginger, finely minced
Pinch of ground cinnamon
3½ cups peeled and seeded fresh guava, sliced into ½-inch pieces
3½ cups strawberries, cut into 4 pieces
1 tablespoon fresh lemon juice
2 tablespoons unsalted butter, cut into pieces

Egg Wash
1 large egg
2 tablespoons cream or half and half
Demerara or raw sugar

1. Preheat the oven to 375 degrees. Lightly dust your work surface with flour and roll 1 dough disk into an 11-inch round. Spray a 9-inch pie pan with nonstick cooking spray. Place the dough round in the prepared pan. Using kitchen scissors, trim the edge of the dough, leaving ¾-inch of overhang. Chill in the refrigerator or freezer for 30 minutes.

2. While the pie crust is chilling, prepare the filling. In a small bowl, combine the sugar and lemon zest. Using your fingers, rub the zest into the sugar until it is well combined. Add the cornstarch, fresh or candied ginger, and cinnamon. Stir to combine.

3. In a medium bowl combine the guava pieces, strawberries, and lemon juice. Stir to combine. Add the sugar mixture and stir gently to combine.

4. Transfer the pie filling into the chilled pastry-lined pan. Place the butter pieces evenly on top of the filling. Roll out the remaining piece of pie dough and cut into strips. Finish the pie by creating a lattice crust with the dough strips (see page 28). You can also use a lattice dough cutter to make your design. In a small bowl, combine the egg and cream. Brush the egg wash on the lattice top and sprinkle the entire top of the pie with raw sugar.

5. Place the pie on a baking sheet and bake for 10 minutes. Reduce the heat to 350 degrees and bake for another 35 minutes or until the lattice crust is browned and the filling is bubbly. Remove pie from the oven and let cool on a rack for at least 1 hour before cutting.

My recipe editor, Terri Milligan, shared this recipe for a special pie she made every fall at her restaurant in Door County, Wisconsin. It was so popular, she made up to 10 pies per day. Chef Terri tosses together apples, pears, and cranberries along with dried apricots and cranberries. To top it all off, she finishes the pie with a spice-scented streusel inspired by the autumn season. This pie pairs perfectly with hot apple cider (cozy fire optional).

Harvest Pie

Makes one 9-inch pie or deep-dish tart

Prep Time: 40 minutes
Baking Time: 50 to 55 minutes

Crust

½ recipe Mary's Favorite Pie Dough, page 30

Filling

¼ cup dried cranberries

¼ cup dried apricots, cut into slivers

½ cup frozen or fresh cranberries

½ cup firmly packed dark brown sugar

⅓ cup granulated sugar

¾ cup apple cider and 3 tablespoons, divided

1 teaspoon ground cinnamon

½ teaspoon ground nutmeg

½ teaspoon ground cloves

2 tablespoons cornstarch

2 pounds apples or a combination of apples and pears, peeled, cored, and cut into ¼-inch slices (about 5 cups)

2 teaspoons fresh lemon juice

1 teaspoon lemon zest

¼ teaspoon salt

Streusel Topping

½ cup firmly packed brown sugar

½ cup rolled oats

½ cup all-purpose flour

½ teaspoon ground cinnamon

½ teaspoon ground ginger

¼ teaspoon ground cloves

¼ teaspoon salt

4 tablespoons (2 ounces) unsalted butter, chilled and cut into small pieces

Garnish

2 teaspoons demerara or raw sugar

1. Lightly dust your work surface with flour and roll the dough into a 12-inch round. Spray a 9-inch deep pie pan or deep tart pan with nonstick cooking spray. If using a tart pan, line the bottom with a round of parchment paper. Place the dough round in the prepared pan and trim the dough side. If making the pie in a pie tin, use kitchen scissors to trim the edge of the dough, leaving ¾-inch of overhang. Crimp or flute the side of the dough. If using a deep tart pan, use a rolling pin or sharp knife to trim the dough flush with the pan side. Refrigerate or freeze the dough-lined pan for 30 minutes while preparing the filling and streusel topping.

2. Preheat the oven to 375 degrees. In a saucepot, combine the dried cranberries, dried apricots, fresh cranberries, brown sugar, granulated sugar, ¾ cup cider, cinnamon, nutmeg, and cloves. Simmer over medium heat until sugar is dissolved.

3. In a small bowl, combine the remaining 3 tablespoons cider with the 2 tablespoons cornstarch. With heat on medium low, drizzle the cornstarch mixture into the dried fruit mixture. Mixture should come to a low boil and thicken. Remove from the heat and cool to room temperature.

4. Place the sliced apples and pears in a large mixing bowl. Toss with lemon juice, lemon zest, and salt. Fold in the room temperature cooked fruit mixture.

5. In a mixing bowl, combine all of the streusel ingredients except the butter. Using a pastry blender, work the cold butter into the dry mixture until it turns into a coarse crumble.

6. Transfer the fruit mixture evenly into the chilled pastry-lined pie or tart pan. Place the streusel evenly on top of the fruit. Sprinkle raw sugar on top of the streusel.

7. Place the pie on a baking sheet. Bake for 50 to 55 minutes or until the streusel turns a light golden brown. Remove the pie from the oven and let rest on a cooling rack for 2 hours before serving.

The Fourth of July is a big deal at my house. Our family loves gathering to watch the fireworks. Such a special day warrants a special pie. When I can, I pick wild blueberries as they have more flavor. In the Midwest, you can also find super fresh berries at the farmers market. I love to fancy up the top of the pie by decorating the crust with stars made of pastry dough. Brush a little egg wash on top and sprinkle some raw sugar for a nicely browned, sparkly crust fitting for a celebration.

Star Spangled Blueberry Pie

Makes one 9-inch pie

Prep Time: 35 minutes
Baking Time: 55 to 60 minutes

Crust
Mary's Favorite Pie Dough, page 30

Filling
8 cups fresh blueberries, washed and dried, divided
⅔ cup granulated sugar
¼ cup cornstarch
¼ teaspoon ground cinnamon
Pinch of allspice
1 tablespoon fresh lemon juice
1 teaspoon vanilla extract

Egg Wash
1 large egg
1 tablespoon cream
Demerara or raw sugar

1. Lightly dust your work surface with flour and roll the dough into an 11-inch round. Spray a 9-inch pie pan with nonstick cooking spray. Place the dough round in the prepared pan. Using kitchen scissors, trim the edge of the dough, leaving a ¾-inch overhang. Crimp or flute the pie edge. Refrigerate or freeze the dough-lined pie pan while preparing the filling.

2. Place 1 cup of berries in a food processor. Add the sugar, cornstarch, cinnamon, and allspice. Pulse to puree the mixture. Transfer the mixture to a small saucepan. Add the lemon juice and vanilla extract. Bring to a boil over medium heat, whisking constantly. The mixture will begin to thicken after a minute or two of boiling.

3. Place the remaining blueberries in a large mixing bowl. Pour the thickened blueberry mixture over the berries and stir gently to combine. Let the filling cool for 10 minutes before filling the pie shell.

4. Preheat the oven to 400 degrees. Remove the pastry-lined pie tin from the refrigerator or freezer. Transfer the cooled filling into the pie shell. Roll the remaining dough disk to a ⅛-inch thickness. Using star cookie cutters, cut out pieces of pie dough and place them decoratively on top of the filling. I like to use different sizes of stars but that's all up to you! Gather up any dough scraps and wrap in plastic wrap. The unused dough can be refrigerated or frozen for another use.

5. Combine the egg and cream in a small bowl. Using a pastry brush, lightly brush the crimped pie edge and the star cutouts. Sprinkle raw sugar over the top of the pie. Place the pie on a baking sheet (this one likes to bubble up) and bake for 30 minutes. Reduce the heat to 350 and bake for another 25 to 30 minutes. Allow the pie to cool on a rack for 2 hours before serving.

You might be surprised to learn that apple pie did not originate in the United States. Apple pie actually originated in England. It was European settlers who brought this beloved pie to the states.

My version is topped with a delicious homemade streusel that I flavor with an exotic blend of spices known as chai. I make my own mix and have included the recipe in my book. Believe me, you will want to keep some homemade chai mix in your pantry. In addition to using it in my apple pie recipe, it makes one delicious chai latte!

Chai-Spiced Streusel Apple Pie

Makes one 9-inch pie

Prep Time: 35 minutes

Baking Time: 60 to 70 minutes

Crust

½ recipe Mary's Favorite Pie Dough

Filling

½ cup (4 ounces) plus 1 tablespoon unsalted butter, divided

8 Granny Smith apples, peeled, cored, and sliced

1½ teaspoons Mary's Homemade Chai Spice Mix, page 218

3 tablespoons all-purpose flour

¼ cup water

½ cup granulated sugar

½ cup firmly packed brown sugar

Streusel

3 tablespoons plus 1 teaspoon unsalted butter, melted

⅓ cup whole oats (not instant)

½ cup all-purpose flour

½ cup granulated sugar

½ teaspoon Mary's Homemade Chai Spice Mix, page 218

¼ teaspoon salt

Egg Wash

1 large egg

1 tablespoon cream

Chai-Spiced Whipped Cream

1½ cups chilled heavy cream

3 tablespoons confectioners' sugar

¼ teaspoon Mary's Homemade Chai Spice Mix, page 218

1. Lightly dust your work surface with flour and roll the dough into an 11-inch round. Spray a 9-inch pie pan with nonstick cooking spray. Place the dough round into the prepared pan. Using kitchen scissors, trim the edge of the dough, leaving a ¾-inch overhang. Crimp or flute the side of the dough and refrigerate or freeze for 30 minutes while preparing the filling and crumble topping.

2. In a large sauté pan, melt 1 tablespoon of the butter. Add the sliced apples and simmer on low heat for 8 to 10 minutes to soften the apples. Turn off the heat and add the spices, tossing apples gently to coat. Transfer the apples to a bowl to let cool.

3. Preheat the oven to 350 degrees. In a sauté pan, melt ½ cup butter. Stir in the flour to form a paste. Add the water and both sugars. Bring to a boil, stirring constantly, then reduce the heat and simmer for several minutes to thicken.

4. Combine all of the ingredients for the streusel either in a food processor or in a mixing bowl. If using a food processor, pulse to combine. If using a mixing bowl, just use your fingers to work the streusel ingredients together. Let the streusel rest for 10 minutes so the melted butter absorbs into the oats.

5. Place the cooled apples in the lined pie pan. Pour the sugar and butter liquid over the apples being careful not to let it run over the side of the pan. If necessary, reheat the butter mixture on low to loosen it up. I like to let the filling settle for a few minutes.

6. Combine the egg and cream. Brush the crust side lightly with the egg wash.

7. Place the pie on a baking sheet. Bake in the preheated oven for 20 minutes. After 20 minutes, top the pie evenly with the streusel. Bake for an additional 40 to 50 minutes or until the streusel is nicely browned. The pie filling may bubble slightly over the rim, but that's okay! Remove the pie from the oven and let cool for 1 hour on a wire rack. While cooling, prepare the chai-spiced whipped cream.

8. To make the chai-spiced whipped cream, place the cream in a chilled bowl of a stand mixer. Using the whip attachment, whip the cream on medium-high speed until soft peaks form. Reduce speed to medium and slowly add the confectioners' sugar and chai spices. Whip until medium peaks form. Serve with the apple pie!

Pineapple pie is very popular in Latin America. The majority of fresh pineapple sold in the world market is grown there. Because the sweetness of pineapple depends on the ripeness of the fruit, I usually start this recipe with only ¼ cup of the granulated sugar. I taste the mixture as it's cooking and add additional sugar as needed. I love making these as individual tartlets so all my guests have their very own mini-pies to enjoy!

Spiced Rum Pineapple Tartlets
Makes eight 4-inch tartlets

Prep Time: 40 minutes
Baking Time: 20 to 22 minutes

Pie Pastry
Mary's Favorite Pie Dough, page 30
or
Pâte Brisée, page 31

Filling
5 cups, packed, fresh cubed pineapple (about 1 large pineapple)
¼ cup to ½ cup granulated sugar, to taste
¼ cup firmly packed light brown sugar
1 cinnamon stick, broken in half
¼ cup cornstarch
1 cup water
½ teaspoon vanilla extract
1 tablespoon dark spiced rum, optional

Garnish
Toasted coconut

1. Lightly dust your work surface with flour. Roll 1 dough disk into a ⅛-inch thickness. Spray eight 4-inch tart pans with nonstick cooking spray. I like to use an oversized muffin tin for this recipe but small tart pans will also work. Cut dough into 6-inch rounds and place in the prepared pans. Continue rolling out the other piece of dough until you have all of the pans lined. Trim and crimp the edges of the tartlets. Refrigerate or freeze the lined pans while preparing the filling. If you have extra pie pastry, simply reform into a disk, wrap in plastic wrap, and freeze for later use.

2. In a medium-sized saucepan, combine the pineapple, ¼ cup granulated sugar, ¼ cup brown sugar, and the broken cinnamon stick. Place on low heat and bring to a simmer.

3. In a small bowl, combine the cornstarch with the water. Stir until completely dissolved.

4. Add the cornstarch mixture to the pineapple. Bring to a low boil and cook, stirring often, until thickened, about 8 minutes. Halfway through give the mixture a taste. If you would like it sweeter, add some or all of the additional granulated sugar.

5. Once the mixture is thick, remove the cinnamon stick and stir in the vanilla extract and the rum, if using. Transfer the mixture to a bowl and let it cool completely. While cooling, blind bake the tartlet pastry.

6. Preheat the oven to 350 degrees. Remove the pastry-lined tartlet pans from the refrigerator or freezer. Place them on a baking sheet to make transferring them to the oven easier. Bake the tartlets for approximately 20 to 22 minutes or until they are lightly browned.

7. Let the tartlet crusts cool for 15 minutes, then remove them from their tartlet pans. Using a spoon, evenly distribute the pineapple filling into the tartlet shells. If desired, sprinkle toasted coconut on top of the tartlets. Serve immediately or refrigerate until ready to serve.

My family is crazy for fresh figs. In the Midwest, fig season runs August through October. The flavor combination in this tart is perfect, especially when I drizzle the top with a local honey. This pie has a lovely sweetness as a result of the honey, *pâté sucrée* pastry crust, and roasted fresh figs. The figs are sprinkled with brown sugar or honey and a touch of fresh rosemary, then roasted to caramelized perfection. My family and friends love this tart and so will yours. I promise!

Roasted Fig Tart with Honey Mascarpone Crème

Makes one 10-inch round tart

Prep Time: 45 minutes

Baking Time: 30 minutes to bake tart shell plus 15 minutes to roast the figs

Crust

Pâte Sucrée, page 32

Roasted Figs

10 ripe fresh Turkish brown or black figs

3 tablespoons brown sugar or honey

3 fresh rosemary sprigs

Filling

16 ounces mascarpone cheese, room temperature

8 ounces goat cheese, room temperature

½ cup plain full-fat Greek yogurt

6 to 8 tablespoons honey to taste plus more for final drizzle

1. On a lightly floured work surface, roll the dough into a 12-inch circle with a ⅛-inch thickness.

2. Spray a 10-inch tart pan with a removable bottom with nonstick cooking spray. Line the bottom of the pan with a round of parchment paper. Place the dough gently in the tart pan. Using your fingers, gently press the dough on the bottom and side of the pan. Using a rolling pin or sharp knife, trim the dough flush with the pan side. This is an easy way to trim the excess dough off the tart pan. Any scraps can be added to any extra dough you have and frozen for future use. Refrigerate or freeze the lined tart pan for 30 minutes so the dough is well chilled. Chilling the dough will help the tart shell keep its shape during baking.

3. Preheat the oven to 350 degrees. The tart shell will be blind baked (baked without filling), then cooled and filled with the mascarpone cream and roasted figs. Remove the lined tart pan from the refrigerator or freezer. Line the chilled tart shell with parchment paper. Place pie weights or dried beans evenly on the parchment paper. Bake until the edges of the crust start to brown, about 15 minutes. Remove from the oven and carefully lift the parchment paper (with the weights) out of the tart pan. Using a fork, make 6 light pricks in the bottom of the crust, being careful not to go all the way through. Return the tart pan to the oven and bake for an additional 10 to 15 minutes or until lightly browned. Remove from the oven and let cool on a wire rack before adding the filling. For more information on blind baking a crust, see page 29.

4. Increase the oven temperature to 400 degrees. Cut the figs in half horizontally. Place the figs, cut side up, on a parchment-lined baking sheet. Sprinkle with brown sugar or brush with honey. Remove the rosemary needles from the rosemary sprig and coarsely chop them. Sprinkle the chopped fresh rosemary on top of the figs. Roast in the oven for about 15 minutes, watching carefully so they do not burn. The figs should become caramelized. Remove from the oven and let the figs cool completely.

5. In a mixing bowl, combine the mascarpone, goat cheese, Greek yogurt, and honey to taste. Mix until well combined.

6. Using a small, offset spatula, spread the filling evenly into the cooled tart shell. Top with the roasted figs, cut side up. Right before serving, drizzle with a little more honey.

When peaches are in season, I'm all in. I can't get enough fresh peaches. In addition to making peach pies from fruit right off the tree, I freeze peeled, sliced peaches for future use. My favorite peaches come from Calhoun County, Illinois, an area famous for its tree-ripened fruit. Situated between the Mississippi and Illinois rivers, this microclimate is a perfect place for peach trees to thrive. If I don't have time to pick the peaches myself, I buy them from a roadside market.

Peachy Peach Pie

Makes one 9-inch lattice crust or double-crust pie

Prep Time: 1 hour and 15 minutes
Baking Time: 1 hour and 5 minutes
Cooling Time: 4 hours

Filling

7 to 8 ripe peaches, peeled, pitted, and sliced (about 2½ pounds)
½ cup granulated sugar
3 tablespoons cornstarch
¼ cup orange juice
Zest of 1 orange
1 teaspoon unsalted butter
1 teaspoon vanilla extract
⅛ teaspoon ground nutmeg
A pinch of salt
2 to 4 tablespoons flour, as needed

Crust

Mary's Favorite Pie Dough, page 30
or
Pâte Brisée, page 31

Egg Wash

1 large egg
2 tablespoons cream
Demerara or raw sugar

1. Prepare the filling before rolling out the pie dough. The filling should be cooled to room temperature before filling the pie. Start by removing the skin from the fresh peaches. I find the best way to remove peach skin is to plunge them into boiling water for 30 to 45 seconds. The timing depends on the size and ripeness of the peaches. Have a bowl of cold ice water ready. Pop those peaches right into the cold water from the boiling water. Their peels should slip off easily. Cut peaches in half and remove the pits.

2. Cut 1 peach into ½-inch dice and place in a small bowl. Slice the remaining peaches and place them in a large mixing bowl.

3. In a small saucepan, combine sugar, cornstarch, orange juice, orange zest, and butter. Cook on medium heat and bring to a boil. Take off the heat and stir in the diced peach pieces. Return the pot to the heat and bring back to a boil. Reduce heat and simmer for 2 to 3 minutes, stirring occasionally. The mixture should become thick and translucent. Remove pot from the heat and let cool for 10 minutes.

4. Add the vanilla extract, nutmeg, and salt to the bowl of sliced peaches. Using a rubber spatula, transfer the cooked peach mixture into the sliced peaches. Gently mix to combine, adding 2 to 4 tablespoons of flour as needed based on the juiciness of the peaches.

5. Preheat the oven to 425 degrees. Lightly dust your surface with flour and roll 1 dough disk into an 11-inch round with a ⅛-inch thickness. Spray a 9-inch pie pan with nonstick cooking spray. Place the dough round in the prepared pan. Using kitchen scissors, trim the edge of the dough, leaving ¾-inch of overhang. Roll out the remaining piece of dough into an 11-inch round.

6. Pile the cooled peach filling into the prepared pie shell. In a small bowl, whisk together the egg and cream. Use the rolled-out dough piece to create either a double-crust or a lattice crust. You'll find details on how to make a lattice crust on page 28.

7. Using a pastry brush, brush the dough side and pastry strips or double-crust with the egg wash. Trim the dough as needed and use your fingers to crimp the dough around the pan side. Sprinkle the top of the pie liberally with the raw sugar.

8. Place the pie on a baking sheet and bake in the middle rack of the oven for 20 minutes. Reduce the heat to 350 degrees and bake for an additional 45 minutes or until the filling begins to bubble and the crust is nicely browned. Remove the pie from the oven and place on a cooking rack. The pie should rest for at least 4 hours before serving.

Cream and Frozen Pies

I'm crazy for whipped cream. These are the pies I turn to when I want to treat my guests—and myself. Decadent and delicious fillings with the bonus of mounds and mounds of whipped cream on top.

Don't skimp when it comes to whipped cream. Making your own perfectly whipped cream is easy if you follow a few rules.

1. Buy the right cream; it's all about the fat content. Whipping cream must be at least 30 percent fat. Heavy cream must be no less than 36 percent fat. Those 6 percentage points of fat make a huge difference in the volume you can achieve.

2. Chill the heavy cream and the bowl. The colder the cream, the better the result. Using a chilled bowl also keeps the cream colder.

3. Incorporate additions such as sugar after the cream begins to hold a soft peak. Adding the sugar too early means you won't get those lovely, high volume peaks of whipped cream.

Don't forget the finishing touches on the recipes in this chapter. Chocolate curls, candied citrus peel, a drizzle of *dulce de leche*; these final garnishes—and more—make these pies extra special.

Usually when I make these pies I am planning a get-together with family and friends. These pies really set the mood, lift spirits, and satisfy the belly. I guess we could call them my trifecta pies!

When I traveled to Argentina, I stayed with a lovely family. There was never a shortage of dulce de leche in the fridge. Most of the time we would spread it on toasted bread or on *facturas*, which are like mini croissants. One day my host brother smeared a healthy tablespoon of dulce de leche on a banana. He asked, "want to give it a try?" At first bite, I knew what a perfect pairing it is. I'm sure he would love this pie as much as I do.

Banana Dulce de Leche Pie

Makes one pie in a 9-inch springform pan

Prep Time: 35 minutes
Baking Time: 8 minutes (for the crust)
Chilling Time: 3 hours

Gingersnap Pie Crust

2 cups finely ground gingersnap cookies, divided

⅓ cup firmly packed brown sugar

6 tablespoons (3 ounces) butter, melted and slightly cooled

Filling

4 ounces cream cheese, softened

4 tablespoons (2 ounces) unsalted butter, softened

2 tablespoons confectioners' sugar

1 teaspoon ground cinnamon

½ teaspoon ground cloves

¼ teaspoon ground nutmeg

1 cup heavy cream

1 cup store-bought dulce de leche
or
1 cup homemade dulce de leche, page 219

3 bananas, sliced

Garnish

1¼ cups heavy cream, chilled

3 tablespoons confectioners' sugar

1 tablespoon cornstarch

2 tablespoons dulce de leche

½ teaspoon vanilla extract

½ cup crushed gingersnap cookies (reserved from making the crust)

Additional dulce de leche for drizzling on top of the pie, optional

1. Prepare the crust by placing 1½ cups of the ground gingersnaps, brown sugar, and butter in a mixing bowl. Reserve the remaining ½ cup crumbs for the final pie garnish. Stir until well combined. Spray a 9-inch springform pan with nonstick cooking spray and line with a round of parchment paper. Using your hands, press the cookie mixture into the bottom and side of the springform pan. Place the lined pan in the refrigerator or freezer for 30 minutes to chill. While chilling, preheat the oven to 350 degrees. Bake the gingersnap crust for 8 minutes. Remove from the oven and let cool before filling.

2. In the bowl of a stand mixer, combine the cream cheese and butter. Beat on medium until fluffy. Add the confectioners' sugar and spices to the cream cheese mixture. Now add the heavy cream and whip the entire mixture until soft peaks form.

3. To assemble the pie: Spread 1 cup dulce de leche evenly on the prepared crust. Place the sliced bananas on top of the dulce de leche then mound the whipped cream cheese mixture on top. Refrigerate the pie for 3 hours to set.

4. When ready to serve, prepare the dulce de leche whipped cream. Place the cream in a chilled bowl of a stand mixer. Using the whip attachment, whip the cream on medium-high speed until soft peaks form. Reduce speed to medium and slowly add the confectioners' sugar and cornstarch followed by the dulce de leche and vanilla extract. Whip until firm peaks form. Mound the dulce de leche whipped cream on top of the chilled pie. Sprinkle the reserved gingersnaps on top of the pie and, if using, drizzle with a bit more dulce de leche.

Contrary to the name, this "icebox" pie was created in 1951 by Betty Cooper of Silver Springs, Maryland for the annual Pillsbury Bake-Off. Legend has it Cooper got the recipe from a friend's mother, Hilda Larson. I give credit to both ladies! The pie has a creamy mousse-like filling, light and airy. I usually make the pie with my favorite pie dough, but it is equally good with an Oreo™ crust. The pie can be made a day ahead and finished with the whipped cream topping just before serving. Believe me, your guests will not be shy about asking for a second piece.

French Silk Pie

Makes one 9-inch pie

Prep Time: 20 minutes
Baking Time: 13 to 24 minutes, depending on pie crust recipe you have selected
Chilling Time: 6 hours

Crust
½ recipe Mary's Favorite Pie Dough, page 30
or
Oreo™ Cookie Crust, page 33

Filling
1 cup heavy cream, chilled
8 ounces bittersweet or semisweet chocolate
4 large eggs
1 cup granulated sugar, divided
1 cup (8 ounces) unsalted butter, softened
2 teaspoons vanilla extract

Topping
1¼ cups heavy cream, chilled
2 tablespoons confectioners' sugar
1 tablespoon cornstarch
1 teaspoon pure vanilla extract

Optional Garnish
Chocolate Curls, page 220
Mary's Easy Hot Fudge Sauce, page 222

1. If using Mary's Favorite Pie Dough, lightly dust your work surface with flour and roll the dough into an 11-inch round. Spray a 9-inch pie pan with nonstick cooking spray. Place the dough round in the prepared pan. Using kitchen scissors, trim the edge of the dough, leaving ¾-inch of overhang. Crimp or flute the side of the dough and refrigerate or freeze for 30 minutes

2. If using the Oreo Crust, spray a 9-inch pie pan with nonstick cooking spray. Place the crust mixture into the pan. Using your fingers, press the mixture on the bottom and side of the pan. I like to use the bottom of a measuring cup or glass to press firmly on the crust mixture. Chill in the refrigerator or freezer for 30 minutes.

3. Preheat the oven to 350 degrees. If using Mary's Favorite Pie Dough, line the chilled pie crust with parchment paper. Fill with pie weights or dried beans. Make sure the weights are evenly distributed around the pan bottom. Bake until the edge of the crust is starting to brown, about 15 to 16 minutes. Remove pie from the oven and carefully lift the parchment paper (with the weights) out of the pan. Using a fork, make 6 pricks in the bottom of the crust. Return pie crust to the oven and bake for 8 minutes. Remove from the oven. If using an Oreo crust, do not use pie weights. Bake the Oreo crust for 13 to 15 minutes. Either crust needs to cool completely before adding the filling. For more information on blind baking a crust, see page 29.

4. Place the cream in the chilled bowl of a stand mixer. Using the whip attachment, whip the cream on medium-high speed until stiff peaks form. Transfer the whipped cream to another bowl and refrigerate while preparing the rest of the filling. You will be using the mixer bowl again so wash and dry it.

5. Place the chocolate in a microwavable bowl. Microwave in 20-second bursts until the chocolate is melted. *(continued)*

French Silk Pie

Continued

6. Fill a pot with water. Place a heat-proof bowl over the water, making sure the water does not touch the bottom of the bowl. Remove the bowl and heat the water. Add the eggs and ½ cup sugar into the bowl and whisk for 2 minutes to combine. When the water reaches a simmer, place the bowl with the eggs on top of the pot. Make sure the water is simmering, not boiling. Whisk the mixture constantly until it reaches a temperature of 160 degrees using an instant-read thermometer. This method ensures that your eggs are at the proper temperature to consume.

7. Using a stand mixer, beat the butter with the remaining ½ cup sugar and vanilla on medium until creamy, about 3 minutes. Scrape the side of the bowl often to make sure all the butter is whipped.

8. Reduce the mixer speed to low and add the chocolate and the egg mixture. Increase the speed to medium and beat for 2 minutes. Remove the bowl from the mixer and fold in the refrigerated whipped cream using a rubber spatula.

9. Spread the filling evenly into the cooled pie crust and cover loosely with plastic wrap. Refrigerate for at least 6 hours or overnight. The pie can be prepared and kept in the refrigerator for up to 3 days.

10. When ready to serve, prepare the whipped cream topping. Place the cream in a chilled bowl of a stand mixer. Using the whip attachment, whip the cream on medium-high speed until soft peaks form. Reduce speed to medium and slowly add the confectioners' sugar followed by the cornstarch and vanilla extract. Whip until fairly stiff. Mound the whipped cream on top of the chilled pie. Garnish with chocolate curls and, if you want even more chocolate, Mary's Hot Fudge Sauce.

who doesn't like a pie of ice cream, fudge sauce, pecans, and Kahlua? *Tip:* Soften the ice cream slightly in the refrigerator 10 to 15 minutes before assembling the pie. About 10 minutes before serving, take the pie out of the freezer and place it in the refrigerator so the pie is easier to slice. Consider making a double recipe of my delicious fudge sauce. Believe me, your guests won't say no to some additional fudge sauce on their pie slice!

Mississippi Mud Ice Cream Pie

Makes one 9-inch pie in a springform pan

Prep Time: 1 hour and 15 minutes
Bake Time: 8 to 10 minutes
Freezing Time: 4 hours plus

Crust

Oreo™ Cookie Crust, page 33

Filling

2 pints vanilla bean ice cream

2 tablespoons coffee-flavored liqueur

¾ teaspoon vanilla extract

½ cup coarsely chopped pecans

2 pints coffee ice cream

Fudge Sauce

4 ounces unsweetened chocolate, coarsely chopped

½ cup firmly packed brown sugar

¼ cup granulated sugar

¾ cup heavy cream

¼ cup light corn syrup

2 tablespoons unsalted butter cut into cubes, room temperature

½ teaspoon vanilla extract

1 tablespoon coffee-flavored liqueur

Topping

1½ cups heavy cream

3 tablespoons confectioners' sugar

3 tablespoons coarsely chopped pecans

Reserved fudge sauce

1. Preheat the oven to 350 degrees. Spray a 9-inch springform pan with nonstick cooking spray. Place the crust mixture into the pan. Using your fingers, press the mixture on the bottom and side of the pan. I like to use the bottom of a measuring cup or glass to press firmly on the crust mixture. Chill in the refrigerator or freezer for 30 minutes. Bake the crust for 8 to 10 minutes. Remove from the oven and let cool on a rack.

2. Once the crust is cool, begin preparing the filling and fudge sauce. Place the vanilla ice cream in a mixing bowl. Allow to soften in the refrigerator for 10 minutes. Mix in 2 tablespoons of the coffee-flavored liqueur and ¾ teaspoon vanilla extract. Spread the ice cream evenly into the chilled baked pie crust. Place the pie in the freezer while preparing the fudge sauce.

3. Prepare the fudge sauce. In a microwaveable bowl, combine the chocolate, brown sugar, granulated sugar, ¾ cup heavy cream, and corn syrup. Microwave in 30-second intervals until the chocolate is melted. Stir until completely smooth. Whisk in the butter, vanilla, and the remaining 1 tablespoon coffee-flavored liqueur.

4. Remove the pie from the freezer. Top the pie with half of the fudge sauce and all of the chopped pecans. Freeze for 1 hour.

5. Begin preparing the final layer of coffee ice cream 45 minutes into the freezing of the fudge layer. Soften the coffee ice cream in the refrigerator for 15 minutes. Spread the coffee ice cream over the pie. If needed, mound the coffee ice cream making a slight "dome" in the pie. Drizzle a little more fudge sauce over the coffee ice cream layer, reserving some to decorate the final pie. Freeze for 2 hours and up to 2 days. If freezing longer than 2 hours, lightly cover the frozen pie with plastic wrap.

6. 2 hours before serving, prepare the whipped cream topping. Place the cream in a chilled bowl of a stand mixer. Using the whip attachment, whip the cream on medium-high speed until soft peaks form. Reduce speed to medium and slowly add the confectioners' sugar. Whip until firm peaks form. Mound the whipped cream on top of the frozen pie.

7. Sprinkle the remaining pecans on top of the whipped cream. Cover very loosely with plastic wrap and freeze for 2 hours. Remove from the freezer 10 minutes before serving. Drizzle with the reserved fudge sauce or serve the fudge sauce on the side. If you like, make a double batch of fudge sauce so your guests have plenty to drizzle on their pie slice!

The key lime from the Florida Keys archipelago is another favorite of mine. The fruit has a distinctive flavor like no other, tart but not acidic, and an aromatic quality that enhances the flavor.

This recipe turns the classic key lime pie into individual tartlets. I especially love the flavors as a sweet ending to a good Chicago steak dinner.

Key Lime Tartlets

Eight to ten 4-inch tartlets

Prep Time: 25 minutes
Baking Time: 17 to 20 minutes
Chilling Time: 2 hours

Crust
Mary's Favorite Graham Cracker Crust, page 34

Filling
½ teaspoon lime zest
3 large egg yolks
4 tablespoons granulated sugar
14 ounces sweetened condensed milk
½ cup (4 ounces) Key lime juice

Topping
1 cup heavy cream, chilled
3 tablespoons confectioners' sugar
1 tablespoon cornstarch
1 teaspoon vanilla extract

1. Spray the bottom and side of the miniature tartlet pans with nonstick cooking spray. Place the graham cracker crust mixture into the pans. Using your fingers, press the mixture on the bottom and side of the pan. Chill in the refrigerator or freezer for 30 minutes. Preheat the oven to 350 degrees.

2. Remove the graham cracker-lined tart pans from the refrigerator or freezer. Bake until the edges are set and the crust is lightly browned, about 5 minutes. Let cool completely on a rack.

3. When the crust is cooled, prepare the filling. In the bowl of a stand mixer using the whip attachment, combine the lime zest, egg yolks, and sugar. Mix at high speed until the mixture lightens in color, approximately 5 minutes. Add the sweetened condensed milk and mix until well combined. Stir in the lime juice. Set the tart pans on a baking sheet. Pour the filling mixture evenly into the lined tartlet pans. Place in the oven and bake for 12 to 15 minutes or until the centers are firm.

4. Remove tartlets from the oven and let them cool on a rack to room temperature. Place tarts in the refrigerator and chill for 2 hours before serving.

5. When ready to serve, prepare the whipped cream topping. Place the cream in a chilled bowl of a stand mixer. Using the whip attachment, whip the cream on medium-high speed until soft peaks form. Reduce speed to medium and slowly add the confectioners' sugar and cornstarch followed by the vanilla extract. Whip until firm peaks form. Mound the whipped cream on top of the chilled tartlets or serve the whipped cream on the side.

Peanut butter takes me back to my childhood when mom would pack a freshly made peanut butter and jelly sandwich into my lunchbox. This scrumptious spread made from ground, dry roasted peanuts, is the perfect ingredient for this silky pie. I take full advantage of the equally scrumptious decorations on top. I drizzle the pie with melted chocolate then add peanut butter cups, chocolate chips, and peanut butter chips. Hello, decadent and delicious.

Peanut Butter Pie

Makes one 9-inch pie

Prep Time: 45 minutes
Baking Time: 12 minutes
Chilling Time: 3 to 6 hours

Crust

Mary's Favorite Graham Cracker Crust, page 34

Filling

8 ounces cream cheese, softened
¾ cup confectioners' sugar
1 cup creamy peanut butter
1 cup heavy cream, chilled
1 teaspoon vanilla extract

Garnish

Bittersweet chocolate, melted
Miniature Reese's Cups™
Peanut butter flavored baking chips
Bittersweet chocolate baking chips

1. Spray a 9-inch pie pan with nonstick cooking spray. Place the crust mixture into the pan. Using your fingers, press the mixture on the bottom and side of the pan. I like to use the bottom of a measuring cup or glass to press firmly on the crust mixture. Chill in the refrigerator or freezer for 30 minutes.

2. Preheat the oven to 325 degrees. Remove the chilled lined pie pan from the refrigerator. Bake in the preheated oven for 12 minutes or until crust is lightly browned. Remove and let cool on a wire rack while preparing the filling.

3. In the bowl of a stand mixer fitted with the paddle attachment, combine the softened cream cheese, confectioners' sugar, and peanut butter. Beat on medium until light and fluffy, about 3 minutes. Transfer the mixture to a mixing bowl. Clean the stand mixer bowl. Place the bowl in the refrigerator or freezer for 15 minutes to cool it down before whipping the cream.

4. Place the heavy cream in the chilled mixer bowl. Using the stand mixer and the whip attachment, beat the cream until soft peaks form. Add the vanilla and continue to whip until fairly stiff. Using a large spatula, gently fold the whipped cream into the peanut butter mixture. Transfer the filling into the cooled pie shell. Freeze the pie for 3 hours or chill in the refrigerator for at least 6 hours.

5. When ready to serve, melt the bittersweet chocolate in a microwave. Let the chocolate cool slightly before drizzling it on top of the pie. Remove the foil from the peanut butter cups. Decorate the top of the pie with the peanut butter cups, peanut butter flavored baking chips, and bittersweet chocolate baking chips.

After exams, my college roommate and I indulged in our favorite hangout's two-for-one ice cream drink special. I always got the Grasshopper. This pie is like an ice cream drink in a chocolate cookie crumb crust. I make this pie even more chocolatey by adding a layer of chocolate ganache between the crust and filling. Top the frozen pie with the whipped cream then pop it back in the freezer for at least an hour to set the cream. I like to garnish the top of the pie with chocolate curls and pieces of Oreo cookies.

Grasshopper Pie

Makes one pie in a 9-inch springform or 9 by 2-inch tart pan

Prep Time: 45 minutes
Freezing Time: 10 hours

Crust

Oreo™ Cookie Crust (regular or mint flavored), page 33

Mint Chocolate Ganache

¾ cup heavy cream

6 ounces bittersweet chocolate, finely chopped

2 tablespoons unsalted butter, cut into cubes

¼ teaspoon mint extract

Filling

40 large (approximately 10 ounces) marshmallows

2¼ cups heavy cream, divided

¼ cup white Crème de Cacao

¼ cup green Crème de Menthe

Green food coloring, as needed

Topping

1¼ cups heavy cream, chilled

3 tablespoons confectioners' sugar

Broken Oreo cookies

Chocolate curls, page 220

1. Spray the springform or tart pan with nonstick cooking spray. Line the pan bottom with a round of parchment paper. Place the crust mixture into the pan. Using your fingers, press the mixture on the bottom and side of the pan. I like to use the bottom of a measuring cup or glass to press firmly on the crust mixture. Chill in the refrigerator or freezer for 30 minutes. The crust for this pie does not need to be prebaked.

2. To prepare the chocolate mint ganache, place ¾ cup heavy cream in a saucepot. Heat on medium heat until small bubbles form on the edge. While the cream is heating, place the finely chopped chocolate and butter in a heat-proof mixing bowl. Add the mint extract to the hot cream, then pour over the chocolate. Let mixture sit for 2 minutes, then stir to combine. The heat of the cream will melt the chocolate. Evenly spread the chocolate ganache mixture on top of the Oreo crust. Place back into the refrigerator or freezer.

3. In a heat-proof bowl, place the marshmallows and 1 cup cream. Place the bowl over a pot of simmering water, making sure the water does not touch the bottom of the bowl. Heat, stirring often with a heat-proof spatula, until the marshmallows are melted. Remove from the heat. Fold in the Crème de Cacao and Crème de Menthe. Cool for 10 minutes.

4. Place the remaining 1¼ cups heavy cream in the bowl of a stand mixer. Using the whip attachment, whip on medium-high speed until stiff peaks form. Using a spatula, fold the marshmallow mixture into the whipped cream. If desired, add a few drops of food coloring to create a soft green color. Transfer the mixture to the prepared pan, evenly covering the ganache layer. Freeze, uncovered, for 1 hour. Cover with plastic wrap or aluminum foil and freeze for an additional 8 hours. The pie can be prepared several days in advance.

5. When ready to serve, prepare the whipped cream garnish. Place the remaining 1¼ cups heavy cream in a chilled bowl of a stand mixer. Using the whip attachment, whip the cream on medium-high speed until soft peaks form. Reduce speed to medium and slowly add the confectioners' sugar. Whip until fairly stiff. Mound the whipped cream on top of the pie. Place the pie back in the freezer and freeze for 1 hour. This will firm up the whipped cream garnish. Remove the springform side or remove from the tart pan and place on a serving platter. Garnish with additional Oreos or chocolate curls.

This is a great make-ahead summer pie that keeps in the freezer for up to 2 days and has the perfect balance of sweet and salty. Who would think pretzels could be turned into such a delicious crust! Pick your berries for this one. Blackberries, raspberries, strawberries? They all work beautifully. I like to make this pie in a deep loaf pan.

Frozen Berry Yogurt Pie with Pretzel Crust

Makes one pie in a 10 by 3 by 5-inch loaf pan

Prep Time: 1 hour and 10 minutes
Baking Time: 8 to 9 minutes
Freezing Time: 4 hours plus

Pretzel Crust

2 cups finely ground pretzel crumbs
10 tablespoons (5 ounces) unsalted butter, melted
⅓ cup granulated sugar

Filling

12 ounces fresh blackberries, raspberries, or strawberries
3 tablespoons granulated sugar
2 tablespoons fresh lemon juice
1½ cups heavy cream
¾ cup sweetened condensed milk
1½ cups plain full-fat Greek yogurt

1. Preheat the oven to 350 degrees. In a mixing bowl, combine the pretzel crumbs, melted butter, and sugar. Mix to combine.

2. Line the loaf pan with parchment paper leaving 3-inches of overhang on the longer sides of the pan. This will make removing the pie from the pan easier. Transfer the crumb mixture to the loaf pan. Press the crumbs firmly around the bottom and sides of the pan. Place the lined pan in the refrigerator or freezer for 30 minutes. This will firm up the butter and keep the crust from sliding down during baking.

3. Bake in the preheated oven for 8 to 9 minutes or until lightly browned. Remove from the oven and let cool on a rack before adding the filling.

4. Place the berries, sugar, and lemon juice in a food processor. Pulse to create a puree. If using blackberries or raspberries, push the mixture through a sieve to remove any seeds. Use the back of a spoon to press the mixture against the sieve so you have a nice, smooth puree.

5. In the bowl of a stand mixer, combine the cream and condensed milk. Whip on medium high until stiff peaks form. Using a rubber spatula, gently fold the yogurt into the cream mixture.

6. Using a large spatula, transfer half of the yogurt filling into the prepared crust. Use a spoon to even out the filling. Drop half of the fruit mixture on top of the filling. Gently pull the spoon through the fruit to create swirls in the yogurt mixture. Repeat with the remaining yogurt mixture and fruit filling. Freeze until firm for 4 hours or up to 2 days. When ready to serve, remove from the freezer and use the parchment paper to lift the frozen pie out of the pan. Let it sit at room temperature for 20 to 30 minutes before serving to make slicing easier.

I first tried a version of this pie at Wildfire Restaurant in Chicago. I fell in love with it immediately. When they took it off the menu, I simply had to create a version of my own. I use a coconut shortbread crust, more coconut, and a bit of banana liqueur for a grownup taste. I made this pie for my good friend Bud, who gave it a thumbs-up seal of approval. That means a lot as Bud is something of a coconut connoisseur.

Coconut Banana Cream Pie

Makes one 8 by 2-inch tart or one 9-inch pie

Prep Time: 30 minutes
Baking Time: 53 minutes
Cooling Time: 1½ hours

Crust

7½ ounces shortbread cookies
(about 2 boxes)

1¼ cups loosely packed unsweetened coconut

2 tablespoons granulated sugar

4 tablespoons (2 ounces) unsalted butter, melted

Filling

1½ cups granulated sugar

1 tablespoon all-purpose flour

¼ teaspoon baking powder

¼ teaspoon salt

3 large eggs

1 cup buttermilk

4 tablespoons (2 ounces) unsalted butter, melted and cooled

1 teaspoon vanilla extract

1 teaspoon banana liqueur or banana extract

5 ounces unsweetened toasted shredded or shaved coconut, divided

Garnish

1¼ cups heavy cream, chilled

3 tablespoons confectioners' sugar

1 tablespoon cornstarch

½ teaspoon banana liqueur or banana extract

2 to 3 bananas, peeled and sliced (select bananas that are not overly ripe)

2 ounces unsweetened shredded or shaved coconut, toasted

1. Preheat the oven to 350 degrees. Spray the tart pan with nonstick cooking spray. Line pan with a round of parchment paper. Using your hands, break up the cookies into small pieces. Place the cookies in the bowl of a food processor along with coconut and sugar. Pulse until small crumbs form, making sure the coconut is fully processed. Add the melted butter and pulse to combine.

2. Spread the crust mixture evenly into the prepared pan. Using your fingers, press the mixture firmly on the bottom and side of the pan. Place in the refrigerator or freezer for 30 minutes to chill. Bake for 12 to 13 minutes in the preheated oven until the crust is lightly browned. Remove from the oven. If there are a few cracks, just use your fingers to press the crust back together while it is still hot. Keep the oven on.

3. In a mixing bowl, whisk together the sugar, flour, baking powder, salt, and eggs. Add the buttermilk, melted butter, vanilla extract, and banana extract or liqueur. Whisk to combine.

4. Evenly sprinkle ½ cup (approximately 3 ounces) of toasted coconut on the bottom of the pie shell. Pour the filling mixture over the coconut. Bake for approximately 40 minutes or until set. The custard filling may jiggle a bit but should be firm to the touch. Remove and let cool on a rack for 1½ hours before completing. The pie can be prepared to this point and refrigerated overnight. Simply finish when you are ready to serve.

5. When ready to serve, prepare the whipped cream. Place the cream in a chilled bowl of a stand mixer. Using the whip attachment, whip the cream on medium-high speed until soft peaks form. Reduce speed to medium and slowly add the confectioners' sugar and cornstarch followed by the banana extract or banana liqueur. Whip until fairly stiff.

6. Place half of the banana slices on top of the cooled custard. Pile the whipped cream on top of the pie and garnish with the remaining sliced bananas and toasted coconut.

When my daughter Rebecca heard I was writing a book on pies, she said "Mom, you *must* include Paloma pie." I had no idea the ingredients were in a favorite cocktail of hers. I got right on it. The grapefruit, lime, and tequila combination is really nice. Rebecca, I hope you approve!

I garnish this pie with homemade candied grapefruit. *Tip:* Remove the peel from a fresh grapefruit before squeezing out the juice. You can use that beautiful peel to make the most delicious, candied grapefruit garnish.

Frozen Paloma Pie

Makes one pie in a 9-inch springform pan or 9 by 2-inch tart pan

Prep Time: 30 minutes
Baking Time: 10 minutes
Freezing Time: 8 hours plus

Crust

Mary's Favorite Graham Cracker Crust, page 34

Filling

1¼ cups heavy cream, chilled

1½ cups freshly squeezed red grapefruit juice

1½ tablespoons fresh lime juice

1 (14 ounce) can sweetened condensed milk

2 to 3 tablespoons tequila blanco

Garnish

¾ cup heavy cream, chilled

3 tablespoons confectioners' sugar

1 teaspoon tequila blanco

Candied grapefruit zest or slices, purchased or make your own, page 217

1. Prepare the graham cracker crust according to my recipe on page 34. Spray the pan bottom with nonstick cooking spray and line it with a round of parchment paper. Using your fingertips, firmly press the crust on the bottom and side of the pan. Refrigerate or freeze the lined pan for 30 minutes. Preheat the oven to 350 degrees. Bake the chilled crust for 10 minutes or until lightly browned. Cool crust completely before filling.

2. If you will be making your own candied grapefruit peel, remove the peel now from your fresh grapefruit. Use a paring knife to make long ¼-inch pieces of grapefruit peel. Now squeeze your juice.

3. Place the chilled whip cream in a chilled bowl of a stand mixer fitted with the whip attachment. Whip until stiff peaks form, about 4 minutes.

4. In a separate bowl, place the grapefruit juice, lime juice, condensed milk, and tequila. Gently fold in half of the whipped cream until just combined. Fold in the remaining cream, being careful not to over mix. You don't want to deflate the whipped cream.

5. Transfer the filling to the graham cracker crust-lined pan. Freeze for at least 8 hours or overnight.

6. When ready to serve, whip the remaining ¾ cup chilled heavy cream. Place the cream in a chilled bowl of a stand mixer. Using the whip attachment, whip the cream on medium-high speed until soft peaks form. Reduce speed to medium and slowly add the confectioners' sugar along with the tequila. Whip until fairly stiff. Top the pie with the whipped cream. Garnish the top of the frozen pie with the whipped cream and candied grapefruit zest or slices.

When I was in grade school, my father took me to a favorite neighborhood ice-cream parlor. I loved going because the ice-cream scoops were square, not round like most places. One time I told him I wanted to try something different, so he ordered me a butterscotch milkshake. I took to it immediately! I had no idea butterscotch was such a divine combination of butter and brown sugar. Of course, I had to make a butterscotch pie. This one's for you, dad.

Butterscotch Tart with Brown Sugar Oatmeal Crust

Makes one 9-inch tart

Prep Time: 1 hour
Baking Time: 25 minutes (for the crust)
Cooling Time: 4 hours

Crust

2 cups old-fashioned rolled oats (not instant)

¼ cup all-purpose flour

¼ cup firmly packed brown sugar

½ teaspoon salt

¼ teaspoon ground cinnamon

6 tablespoons (3 ounces) unsalted butter, melted and slightly cooled

Filling

6 tablespoons (3 ounces) unsalted butter

6 tablespoons all-purpose flour

1½ cups firmly packed brown sugar

2 cups whole milk

¼ teaspoon salt

3 large egg yolks, room temperature

1 teaspoon vanilla extract

Cream Cheese Whipped Cream Topping and Garnish

4 ounces cream cheese, softened to room temperature

1 cup heavy whipping cream, chilled

3 tablespoons confectioners' sugar

1 teaspoon vanilla extract

½ cup crumbled Heath™ bar (approximately 2 candy bars)

1. In the bowl of a food processor, combine the oats, flour, brown sugar, salt, and cinnamon. Pulse until the oats are coarsely chopped. With the processor on, add the butter slowly through the feed tube while pulsing, until the mixture is moistened and holds together.

2. Spray the bottom and side of a 9-inch tart pan with a removable bottom with nonstick cooking spray. Line the pan with a round of parchment paper. Transfer the crust mixture to the prepared tart pan. Using your fingers, press the crumbs firmly into the bottom and up the side of the pan. Refrigerate or freeze for 30 minutes before baking.

3. While chilling, preheat the oven to 350 degrees. Place the chilled lined tart pan on a baking sheet. Bake for approximately 25 minutes or until lightly browned. Remove and let cool on a rack while preparing the filling.

4. In a saucepan, melt the 6 tablespoons of butter. When melted, remove from heat and add the flour. Stir with a heat proof spatula until smooth. Add the brown sugar and return to the heat. Slowly add the milk and salt, stirring constantly. Reduce heat to medium and cook, stirring constantly, until the mixture thickens and bubbles on the side of the pan. Reduce the heat to low and cook for 2 more minutes, again stirring constantly. Remove from the heat.

5. In a mixing bowl, whisk the egg yolks for 1 minute. Add 1 cup of the hot mixture and whisk to combine. This will temper the eggs. Slowly transfer the egg mixture back into the milk mixture. Bring the mixture back to a low boil, whisking constantly, for 2 minutes. Remove from the heat. Stir in the vanilla and pour into the cooled crust.

6. Refrigerate the pie for 4 hours or overnight. When ready to serve, prepare the whipped cream topping. Place the room temperature cream cheese in the bowl of a stand mixer fitted with the whip attachment. Whip until fluffy. Add the cream and whip on medium-high speed until soft peaks form. Reduce speed to medium and slowly add the confectioners' sugar followed by the vanilla extract. Whip until firm peaks form. Mound the whipped cream on top of the chilled pie. Sprinkle the top of the pie with crushed Heath bar.

Savory Pies and Galettes

Not all pies have to be sweet. There's a scrumptious, savory side to pies as well. The recipes in this chapter are all on the savory side and are perfect for lunch or dinner.

My turkey pot pie is a wonderful comfort food and the perfect recipe for all that leftover Thanksgiving turkey. No turkey? No problem. Chicken will do. I never make just one of these pies as I like to have a few in the freezer to pop in the oven for an impromptu meal.

Savory pies are a great place to pay respect to my European lineage. My Guinness™ beef puff pastry pot pie is an ode to my Irish heritage. My butternut squash pasta pie is an ode to my Italian side (I want to spread the love to both sides of the family). The cheesy turkey tamale pie gives some love to my husband's side of the family. This chapter is one of the few times I encourage you to use store-bought crust. Homemade puff pastry is delicious but there are some great premade, frozen puff pastries that make some of these recipes a snap.

This is a chapter to dive into and expand your basic pie-making skills. After all, who wouldn't like some pie as the main course for dinner?

A galette is a rustic French tart with dough rolled out in a free form. You can have a lot of fun with this tart as it doesn't have to be shaped perfectly. In fact, imperfections give a galette character— the perfect pie for an imperfect cook. Just roll out your favorite dough and spread the filling in the middle. Fold up the edge and pinch the side to make pleats. Galettes are popular for ease of creation and versatility. For this filling, feel free to use your favorite combination of mushrooms. Make it your own!

Spinach and Mushroom Galette
Makes one 9-inch round galette

Prep Time: 45 minutes
Baking Time: 35 to 40 minutes

Herb Cornmeal Pastry

2½ cups all-purpose flour

⅔ cup yellow cornmeal (not stone ground)

2 teaspoons sugar

1 teaspoon salt

2 teaspoons finely chopped fresh rosemary

2 teaspoons finely chopped thyme leaves

¾ cup (6 ounces) unsalted butter, chilled and cut into small pieces

¼ cup olive oil

4 to 6 tablespoons ice water, as needed

Filling

4 ounces shiitake mushrooms, stems removed and discarded

6 ounces cremini mushrooms

1 tablespoon olive oil

2 shallots, finely chopped

2 garlic cloves, minced

1 pound washed and dried baby spinach leaves

¼ teaspoon salt

⅛ teaspoon white pepper

Pinch of red pepper flakes

1¼ cups whole ricotta, drained

2 teaspoons finely chopped fresh rosemary

2 teaspoons finely chopped thyme leaves

1¼ cups shredded Swiss or Gruyère cheese

Egg Wash

1 large egg

1 tablespoon heavy cream

1. In the bowl of a food processor, combine the flour, cornmeal, sugar, salt, and herbs. Pulse to combine. With the processor on, slowly add the cubed chilled butter, pulsing to combine. With the processor on, add the olive oil and enough of the water through the feed tube to make a dough that comes together. Place the dough on a work surface and form into a disk. Wrap in plastic wrap and refrigerate while making the filling.

2. Preheat the oven to 375 degrees. Thinly slice both types of mushrooms. In a large sauté pan, heat 1 tablespoon olive oil. Add the shallots and sauté until translucent. Add the garlic and sauté for 30 seconds. Add the mushrooms and sauté for 1 minute until slightly cooked. Pile the spinach leaves on top of the vegetables and cover. Cook on low heat until just wilted, about 2 to 3 minutes. Season with salt, white pepper, and a pinch of red pepper flakes. Remove from heat and let cool for 15 minutes.

3. Roll out the dough on a lightly floured piece of parchment paper. The galette can be made as a 12-inch round. Use the parchment to lift the dough onto a baking sheet.

4. Place the ricotta in a strainer over a bowl. Let the ricotta sit in the strainer for 15 minutes to remove excess liquid. Discard the liquid and place the drained ricotta in a mixing bowl. Add the chopped rosemary and thyme leaves and mix to combine. Using a small offset spatula, spread the ricotta cheese mixture on the prepared crust leaving a 1½-inch border.

5. Pile the vegetable mixture evenly on top of the ricotta. Sprinkle the grated Swiss or Gruyère cheese evenly over the vegetable mixture.

6. In a small bowl, combine the egg and cream. Using your fingers, fold the edge over the filling, pinching the dough as you go to create pleats. Using a pastry brush, lightly brush egg wash on top of the pinched dough.

7. Bake until the crust has browned and cheese is melted, about 35 to 40 minutes. Remove from the oven and slide the galette off of the parchment paper to a cooling rack. Serve warm or at room temperature.

Here is what you get when mixing my Italian heritage with the bounty of our farm! An unusual take on pie made with pasta and an autumn favorite, butternut squash. The cooked rigatoni are placed vertically in a springform pan with a delicious butternut squash puree poured over. Add a little freshly picked sage, frizzled for a crispy topper, and you have the perfect fall dinner.

Butternut Squash and Rigatoni Pie with Frizzled Sage

Makes one 9-inch pie in a springform pan

Prep Time: 50 minutes
Baking Time: 30 minutes

4 cups cubed raw butternut squash (about one 3 pound squash)

2 tablespoons olive oil

¼ teaspoon salt

⅛ teaspoon pepper

5 ounces crumbled blue cheese

8 ounces fresh mozzarella cheese, diced into small pieces

1 large egg

½ cup whole milk

1 pound dry large rigatoni pasta

1 tablespoon unsalted butter

¾ cup chopped onion

1 garlic clove, minced

2 to 3 cups chicken or vegetable stock, as needed

½ teaspoon smoked paprika

¼ teaspoon grated nutmeg

A generous pinch of crushed red pepper flakes

1 tablespoon finely chopped fresh sage leaves, about 3 leaves

¼ teaspoon salt

⅛ teaspoon ground white pepper

⅔ cup shredded mozzarella cheese

Six ¼-inch rounds of fresh mozzarella

Frizzled Sage Leaves

1 tablespoon unsalted butter

12 fresh sage leaves

1. Preheat the oven to 400 degrees. Line a baking sheet with aluminum foil and spray lightly with nonstick cooking spray. Spray a 9-inch springform pan with nonstick cooking spray. Line the pan with a round of parchment paper.

2. Prepare the squash puree. Peel, remove the seeds, and cut squash into ½-inch cubes. Place the squash in a mixing bowl and toss with the olive oil, salt, and pepper. Transfer the squash in a single layer to the prepared baking sheet. Roast for 15 minutes or until soft. Let cool slightly then transfer to a food processor. Add the blue cheese, 8 ounces diced fresh mozzarella, egg, and milk. Pulse until the mixture is pureed. Set aside.

3. While the squash is roasting, cook the pasta. The pasta can be slightly underdone as it will cook again in the pie. Drain and rinse under cool water. Pat dry with a paper towel.

4. In a large skillet, melt the butter over medium heat. Add the onion and cook until softened but still translucent, about 4 minutes. Add the garlic and cook, stirring often, for 1 minute. Add the squash puree, 2 cups of stock, smoked paprika, nutmeg, red pepper flakes, and chopped sage. Whisk to combine and simmer for 2 minutes. If the sauce is too thick, thin with a little more of the stock. Season to taste with salt and pepper.

5. Spread ⅓ cup of the sauce in the bottom of the prepared springform pan. Stack the pasta vertically into the pan. Try to make the pasta very compact. Pour the remaining puree over the pasta making sure to get sauce into the rigatoni holes. Cover the top with the shredded mozzarella cheese. Place on a baking sheet and bake in the oven for 15 minutes. Place the fresh mozzarella slices on top and bake for another 15 minutes or until brown and sauce is bubbling. Let sit for 20 minutes before removing the side of the pan and serving.

6. While the pie is baking, prepare the frizzled sage. In a small sauté pan, melt the remaining 1 tablespoon butter. When melted, reduce the heat to medium low and add the whole sage leaves. Cook for 1 minute then carefully flip the leaves. You want them crisp, not burnt. Remove the leaves and place on a paper towel to drain. Decorate the top of the finished pie with the frizzled sage leaves.

I have many fond memories of shopping with mom and my brother Erik. After the errands, we'd stop at Bakers Square for chicken pot pie, my brother's favorite. Later on, after a Thanksgiving dinner while putting leftovers away, it came to me. How about making my own pot pie recipe with turkey? The next day, we enjoyed individual turkey pot pies. We also made a few extra to tuck in the freezer to bake and enjoy regardless of the season. Whether you use chicken or turkey, this recipe is sure to be a total hit.

Turkey Pot Pie

Makes two 9-inch pies (serving 6 to 8 each) or 12 individual pies

Prep Time: 40 minutes

Baking Time: Large pie 45 to 50 minutes (individual pies 25 to 30 minutes)

Filling

1 tablespoon olive oil

1 tablespoon unsalted butter

2 medium potatoes, peeled and cut into 1-inch pieces

3 medium carrots, peeled and cut into ½-inch slices

1 medium onion, finely chopped

1 celery rib, diced

2 garlic cloves, minced

6 tablespoons all-purpose flour

3 cups chicken or turkey stock

5 cups cubed cooked turkey

⅔ cup frozen peas

½ cup heavy cream

2 tablespoons white wine

1 tablespoon minced fresh parsley

Leaves from 3 fresh sprigs of thyme

¼ teaspoon pepper

Salt to taste

Crust

2 packages (15 ounces each) refrigerated pie dough or a double batch of Mary's Favorite Pie Dough, page 30

Egg Wash

1 large egg

1 tablespoon cream

1. In a Dutch oven or large skillet, heat the olive oil and butter over medium heat. Add the potato, carrot, onion, and celery. Sauté until tender, about 8 minutes. If using leftover vegetables and potato, add them to the skillet to reheat. Add the garlic and cook for 1 minute to soften. Stir in the flour. Stir the mixture, using a heat-resistant spatula or wooden spoon, until the vegetables are coated with the flour. Add the chicken or turkey stock and stir to combine.

2. Bring mixture to a boil. Reduce to a simmer and cook, stirring often, until the mixture thickens. Add the turkey, peas, ½ cup heavy cream, white wine, parsley, thyme leaves, pepper, and salt to taste. Cool mixture before placing in the pastry-lined pie plans.

3. Lightly dust your work surface with flour. You are making two 9-inch pies so you will need 4 disks of dough. Roll out 1 disk of dough into an 11-inch round. Spray a 9-inch pie pan with nonstick cooking spray. Place the dough round in the prepared pan. Using kitchen scissors, trim the edge of the dough, leaving ¾-inch of overhang. Repeat with another disk of dough and another 9-inch pie pan. To make individual pies, check out the notes at the end of this recipe!

4. If baking immediately, preheat the oven to 375 degrees. Divide the cooled turkey mixture evenly between the 2 pastry-lined pie pans. Roll the remaining 2 disks of dough into 11-inch rounds. Place dough rounds on top of each pie. Press firmly on the pie dough edge to adhere the 2 pieces then trim and crimp the pie edge.

5. In a small bowl, combine the egg and tablespoon of cream. Brush egg wash over the top pastry and make two slits on top of each pie. This will help release steam as the pies bake.

6. Place pies on a baking sheet and bake for 45 to 50 minutes or until golden brown. Let pies rest for 10 minutes before serving.

Individual Pie Variation: Make individual pot pies using 4-inch pie pans or large muffin tins. Prepare the recipe as described, using the smaller pie pans or oversized muffin tins. The recipe will make approximately 12 individual pies. If serving immediately, bake at 375 degrees for approximately 25 to 30 minutes. If baking from a frozen state, bake at 375 degrees for 40 minutes. An instant-read thermometer inserted in the center of the pies should read 165 degrees.

Freezer Option: Wrap unbaked pies with foil and freeze for up to 3 months. When ready to use, preheat the oven to 425 degrees. Remove from the freezer and discard foil wrapping. Wrap new foil only around the pie crust edge. Place pie on a baking sheet. Bake for 30 minutes. Reduce oven temperature to 350 degrees and remove foil. Bake an additional 40 minutes or until golden brown and a thermometer inserted in the center reads 165 degrees. Let the pie rest for 10 minutes before serving.

I may have grown up Italian, but I was lucky enough to have friends who introduced me to the wonderful world of tamales. When they are homemade, nothing is better. I've incorporated the classic tamale flavor profile into this lovely pie. The crust for the pie is made with cornmeal and diced chiles, for a little heat. You can also use shredded or pulled pork in the recipe. If I have to choose between a tamale or my tamale pie, I would hands down go for the tamale pie!

Tamale Pie with Chile Cornmeal Crust

Makes one pie in a 9-inch-deep pie pan or cast iron skillet

Prep Time: 45 minutes
Baking Time: 35 to 40 minutes

Cornmeal Crust
1½ cups cold water
1½ cups fine yellow cornmeal
2 cups boiling water
1 teaspoon salt
1 (4 ounce) can diced green chiles, well-drained

Filling
2 cups shredded cooked chicken or turkey
1 (10 ounce) can enchilada sauce
2 tablespoons chili powder
2 teaspoons smoked paprika
1 teaspoon ground cumin
A pinch of cayenne pepper
¾ teaspoon salt
¼ teaspoon ground black pepper
⅔ cup diced red bell pepper
1 can (15 ounces) black beans, drained
2 tablespoons chopped fresh cilantro
4 ounces shredded cheddar or Monterey Jack cheese

Garnish
Diced avocado
Pomegranate seeds
Salsa
Crumbled queso fresco or cotija cheese

1. Preheat the oven to 375 degrees. In a bowl, combine the cold water and cornmeal. Stir to combine.

2. In a medium pot, bring the additional 2 cups of water to a boil along with the 1 teaspoon of salt. With the water boiling, slowly whisk in the cornmeal mixture. Cook, whisking constantly, until the liquid is absorbed, about 7 minutes. Remove from the heat and stir in the diced chiles.

3. Spray a 9-inch-deep dish pie pan or cast iron skillet with nonstick cooking spray. Transfer the cooked cornmeal mixture to the pan and evenly pat it into the pan bottom and side. I find that using the back of a large spoon works well to even out the cornmeal mixture.

4. Now it's time to make the filling. In a mixing bowl, combine the shredded turkey or chicken, enchilada sauce, chili powder, smoked paprika, cumin, cayenne, salt, and pepper. Stir in the red pepper, black beans, and cilantro. Transfer the mixture to the prepared pie pan and spread out evenly. Sprinkle the 4 ounces of cheese over the top of the filling.

5. Place the filled pie on a baking sheet. Bake in the preheated oven for 35 to 40 minutes or until the pie is bubbling and the cheese is golden brown. Remove from the oven and let rest for 10 minutes before serving. Serve with any (or all!) of the garnishes listed.

When I was pregnant with my daughter Madeline, for whatever reason, I couldn't eat enough carrots. As a youngster, carrots were one of Madeline's favorite vegetables.

When I make my Carrot Feta Galette she is always top of mind, and it remains one of her favorite dishes. I make this colorful tart in the form of a rustic galette with small, multi-colored organic carrots. I add a generous helping of crumbled feta cheese and fresh dill, which gives the galette a savory, herb-y flavor.

Carrot and Feta Galette

Makes two 8 by 5-inch rectangular galettes or one 12-inch round galette

Prep Time: 30 minutes
Baking Time: 30 to 40 minutes

Crust

½ recipe Mary's Favorite Pie Dough, page 30
or
½ recipe Pâte Brisée, page 31

Carrots

1½ pounds multi-colored carrots, peeled but kept whole
2 tablespoons olive oil
Salt and freshly ground black pepper

Feta Filling

1¼ cups (10 ounces) crumbled and packed feta cheese
2 tablespoons fresh lemon juice
1 garlic clove, minced
¼ cup olive oil
¼ cup lightly packed chopped Italian parsley
2 tablespoons chopped fresh dill
A few grinds of fresh ground pepper

Egg Wash

1 large egg
1 tablespoon cream

Garnish

Fresh dill sprigs

1. Preheat the oven to 400 degrees. Slice the carrots in half lengthwise and place, cut side down, on a parchment-lined baking sheet. Drizzle carrots with the olive oil and season lightly with salt and pepper. Roast for 8 minutes if using smaller carrots and 10 minutes if using larger ones. Remove from the oven and let cool while preparing the filling. Reduce oven temperature to 350 degrees.

2. In the bowl of a food processor, combine all the filling ingredients. Pulse until the feta mixture is fairly smooth.

3. On a lightly floured work surface, roll out the dough into a ⅛-inch thickness. If using larger carrots, roll the pastry into a 13-inch round. If using smaller carrots, divide the pastry in half and roll each piece into 9-by 6-inch rectangles. Place the pastry on a new parchment-lined baking sheet.

4. Using a small offset spatula, spread the feta mixture evenly on the pastry, leaving a ¾-inch border on all sides. Place the carrots on the feta mixture. Carefully fold the dough edges, crimping the pastry as needed with your fingers.

5. In a small bowl, whisk the egg with the cream. Using a pastry brush, brush the sides of the dough with the egg wash. Bake in the preheated oven. The smaller rectangular galettes will be done in approximately 30 minutes. The larger round galette will take approximately 40 minutes. The galettes are done when the crust turns a lovely golden brown color.

6. Remove from the oven and garnish with additional fresh dill sprigs. The galette can be served warm or at room temperature.

This popular Greek savory pie is one of my favorites. I love its flaky phyllo dough and filling of spinach and feta cheese. This pie is much easier to make than you think! I often serve it as a side dish with lamb, but spanakopita can easily stand alone as the main dish. Serve with a salad and you are set. The pie also makes for a beautiful presentation with its phyllo "flowers."

Spanakopita Pie

Makes one 9-inch pie

Prep Time: 50 minutes

Baking Time: 45 to 50 minutes

Filling

2 tablespoons olive oil

½ cup finely chopped scallions (white and tender greens parts)

2 garlic cloves, minced

10 ounces cleaned baby spinach

½ teaspoon salt

3 tablespoons chopped fresh oregano

¼ cup finely chopped Italian parsley

1 tablespoon chopped fresh dill

½ cup breadcrumbs

2 tablespoons pine nuts

1 teaspoon grated lemon zest

8 ounces feta cheese, crumbled

¼ cup (1 ounce) finely grated Parmesan cheese

A generous grind of black pepper

2 large eggs

1 large egg yolk

Phyllo Crust and Flowers

1¼ cups (10 ounces) unsalted butter, melted and slightly cooled

16 sheets (13 by 17-inch) frozen phyllo, thawed overnight in the refrigerator

1. Heat the 2 tablespoons of olive oil in a large skillet over medium heat. When hot, add the scallions and sauté, stirring occasionally, for 1 minute. Add the garlic and cook, stirring constantly, for 30 seconds. Add the spinach and salt. Cover the pan and reduce the heat to low. Cook for approximately 2 minutes or until the spinach wilts. Transfer the mixture to a mixing bowl and let cool.

2. Preheat the oven to 375 degrees. Add the oregano, parsley, dill, breadcrumbs, pine nuts, lemon zest, crumbled feta, Parmesan, and black pepper to the spinach mixture. Stir gently to combine. Combine the eggs and egg yolk in a small bowl and whisk until combined. Add the eggs to the spinach mixture and toss gently to combine.

3. Brush a 9-inch pie pan with enough of the melted butter to just coat. Unroll the phyllo dough and place on a kitchen towel. Cover the top of the phyllo with another kitchen towel. This will help keep the phyllo from drying out. Place 1 piece of phyllo dough on your work surface. Brush the dough evenly with butter on one side. Transfer to the pan, arranging butter side up and slightly off-center so the long side of the dough comes up over the side of the pan. You should have a good 3-inch overhang of phyllo. Rotate the pan slightly and repeat with another sheet of dough, again having an overhang of phyllo. Continue this process, rotating the pan as you go, until you use 12 sheets of phyllo dough. You want to have a 3-inch overhang around the entire circumference of the pie plate. Don't worry if it is not beautiful. The dough will be pulled up over the filling soon!

4. Transfer the spinach mixture to the phyllo-lined pie pan. Use your hands to bring the phyllo up around the edge of the pan. Crinkle the phyllo so it resembles loose flowers. A round center of spinach filling will remain exposed.

5. The remaining 4 sheets of phyllo will be used to make beautiful decorative "flowers." Brush one piece of dough with butter. Cut in half. Crinkle each half into a flower shape and place on the edge of the pan. Continue with the remaining dough and butter to make a total of 8 flowers.

6. Place the pie on a baking sheet and bake for 45 to 50 minutes or until the filling is set and the phyllo is nicely browned. Remove from the oven and let the pie rest for 10 minutes before cutting.

I learned to make Turkish Borek from my dear friend Mehmet. Phyllo dough is filled with seasoned ground lamb, rolled into long "ropes" and arranged in spirals in a cast iron skillet. This unusual pie explodes with exotic Middle Eastern flavors. When working with frozen phyllo dough, be sure to thaw overnight. Keep thawed phyllo sheets covered with a damp tea towel and work with one sheet at a time. Use exactly the spice mix called for. If you can't find ground lamb, substitute good quality ground beef or ground sirloin.

Turkish Borek with Spiced Lamb

Makes one 9-inch pie in a cast iron skillet

Prep Time: 1 hour
Baking Time: 40 to 45 minutes

Filling

⅓ cup pine nuts

2 tablespoons olive oil

1 cup finely diced onion

2 garlic cloves, minced

1¼ pounds ground lamb or lean ground beef

1½ teaspoons ground cumin

¾ teaspoon each ground coriander, ground cinnamon, and smoked paprika

½ teaspoon allspice

¼ to ½ teaspoon red pepper flakes (depending on the amount of heat you like)

1½ teaspoon salt

½ teaspoon black pepper

⅓ cup currants or raisins

1 cup tomato puree

¼ cup water

Yogurt Egg Wash

2 large eggs

¼ cup plain full-fat Greek yogurt

4 tablespoons (2 ounces) unsalted butter, melted

Cast Iron Skillet Prep

2 tablespoons softened unsalted butter

Pastry

16 sheets phyllo pastry

3 tablespoons unsalted butter, melted and slightly cooled

3 tablespoons white sesame seeds

Lemon Yogurt Sauce

1 cup (8 ounces) plain Greek yogurt

1 garlic clove, minced

Zest of 1 lemon

1 tablespoon lemon juice

1 to 2 tablespoon extra-virgin olive oil

Salt and freshly ground pepper, to taste

1. Dry roast the pine nuts in a cast iron skillet. Place the pine nuts in the skillet and heat on medium heat until the pine nuts turn golden brown. The pine nuts can burn quickly so keep an eye on them as they roast. Remove them immediately from the skillet so they stop roasting. Let the skillet cool down. You will be using it later to place the formed Borek in. Cook the filling in a different skillet so you have your cast iron skillet ready.

2. In a clean large sauté pan, heat the olive oil on medium heat. Add the onion and sauté until translucent, about 2 to 3 minutes. Add the minced garlic and sauté for another 30 seconds. You do not want to burn the garlic.

3. Now add the lamb or beef and cook until it is evenly browned. Use a large spoon or heat-proof spatula to break up the meat as it cooks.

4. Once the meat is evenly browned, add the spices, salt, pepper, currants, pine nuts, tomato puree, and water. Stir the mixture so it is evenly combined. Cook on low heat for 5 minutes or until the liquid is reduced. Once the filling is ready, remove the skillet from the burner and let cool. The filling must be completely cool before assembling the phyllo dough sheets.

5. While the filling is cooling, prepare the egg wash. In a small bowl, combine eggs, ¼ cup Greek yogurt, and 4 tablespoon melted butter. Use a fork to gently whip the mixture until it is combined.

6. Prepare your cast iron skillet. Brush the 2 tablespoons of melted butter on the bottom and side of a 9-inch cast iron skillet. Set aside.

7. Now you are ready for assembly! You will be placing the filling on 3 sheets of phyllo then rolling the phyllo into tight "ropes." The ropes will then be coiled (like a snake) and transferred to the prepared cast iron pan. It sounds harder than it is! Once you get that first rope done, you'll see how easy it is.

8. Unwrap and unroll the phyllo pastry. Place the pastry on a tea towel and cover with another towel to keep the dough from drying out. Make sure to have your yogurt egg wash ready. Place a sheet of phyllo on your work surface. Brush the top with some of the yogurt egg wash. It's fine if it is not completely covered with wash. Just give it a nice brushing across the surface. Top with another piece of phyllo and brush with the wash. Continue the process with 1 more phyllo sheet and wash. *(continued)*

Turkish Borek with Spiced Lamb

Continued

9. Place ⅓ of the cooled meat mixture across the bottom of the longest side of the phyllo. It should go completely across the bottom and go up about 1½ inches. Now, roll up the pastry into a rope, trying to keep it fairly firm and tight. Continue this process to make 3 more "ropes" of meat-filled pastry. You will end up with 4 long ropes of filled phyllo.

10. It's time to form the ropes into the Borek. Preheat your oven to 375 degrees. Cut each phyllo rope in half. Carefully form each piece of stuffed phyllo into a spiral. Place 1 of the spirals in the middle of the prepared cast iron pan. Now place the remaining 7 spirals around the circumference of the pan. Brush the top of the phyllo with the remaining 2 tablespoons of melted butter and sprinkle evenly with the sesame seeds.

11. Bake in the preheated oven until golden brown, about 40 to 45 minutes. While it is baking, prepare the lemon yogurt sauce. In a mixing bowl, combine the 1 cup Greek yogurt with the minced garlic, lemon juice, lemon zest, and olive oil. Season to taste with salt and pepper.

12. Remove the baked Borek from the oven and let rest for 10 minutes before slicing. This is a great rustic-type dish. I love serving it directly to my guests in the cast iron skillet. Half the fun of this dish is showing off the finished product. Serve with a dollop of the lemon yogurt sauce.

Although my maiden name is Papaleo, I learned I also have Irish heritage. Off to Ireland I went to immerse myself in all things Irish–the culture, customs, and the cuisine. I spent a delicious time enjoying local foods, and of course, a little (okay a lot!) of Guinness™. I also discovered Guinness is not only for drinking. It makes a delicious and rich addition to my beef pot pie filling. I make it "fancy" by topping the pie with beautifully crisp puff pastry.

Guinness Beef Pot Pie with Puff Pastry Topping
Makes one 2-quart casserole

Prep Time: 40 minutes
Cooking and Baking Time:
1 hour 20 minutes

Filling

⅓ cup all-purpose flour

1 teaspoon salt, divided

½ teaspoon black pepper

2½ pounds boneless beef chuck, cut into 2-inch cubes

4 tablespoons olive oil, divided

1 medium onion, peeled and cut into ¼-inch dice

2 celery stalks, cut into ¼-inch dice

3 garlic cloves, minced

2 tablespoons brown sugar

1 tablespoon Worcestershire sauce

1 bay leaf

1½ teaspoons dried thyme

1 teaspoon dried rosemary

1 (11 ounce) bottle Guinness beer

1 (8 ounce) can tomato paste

3½ cups beef broth

2 cups washed unpeeled red potatoes, cut into ½-inch dice

2½ cups peeled carrots, cut into ¼-inch dice

1 cup frozen peas, thawed

1 tablespoon chopped Italian parsley

2 tablespoons cornstarch dissolved in ¼ cup water

Pastry Top

1 sheet frozen puff pastry, thawed

Egg Wash

1 tablespoon heavy cream

1 large egg

1. Combine the flour, ½ teaspoon salt, and ½ teaspoon black pepper in a large ziplock bag. Place the cubed beef in the bag and shake to cover meat with flour. Remove floured meat and set aside while preparing a Dutch oven. Discard the remaining flour.

2. Heat 2 tablespoons of oil in a Dutch oven over medium heat. Add half the meat and sear on all sides. Remove and place in a clean bowl. Add the additional oil and brown the remaining meat. Place the meat in the bowl with the other half of the seared beef.

3. In the pot used for searing the beef, add the onion, celery, garlic, and brown sugar. Cook on medium-low heat until the onions are translucent, about 4 minutes. Add the Worcestershire sauce, bay leaf, thyme, and rosemary. Stir to combine. Add the beer, tomato paste, beef broth, and remaining ½ teaspoon salt. Cover and simmer for 45 minutes, stirring occasionally.

4. Remove the bay leaf from the stew mixture. Add the potatoes and cook for 15 minutes on medium heat. Add the carrots and cook until carrots and potatoes are tender, about 15 more minutes. Stir in the thawed green peas and the parsley.

5. Combine the cornstarch and water in a small bowl. On medium heat, drizzle filling with enough of the cornstarch mixture to thicken. The sauce should coat the back of a spoon. You may not need all of the cornstarch mixture. Simmer for an additional 3 minutes. Remove from the heat and transfer the beef filling to a clean baking dish or Dutch oven. Let it cool for 30 minutes. You don't want the filling to be too hot when you top it with the puff pastry.

6. Preheat the oven to 375 degrees. Cut out a piece of puff pastry the size of the baking dish top. Place on top of the stew. Combine the cream and egg in a small bowl. Brush the pastry with the egg wash mixture. If desired, cut out shapes with the puff pastry scraps and place on top of the puff pastry top. Remember to brush any decorations with egg wash as well so they get nice and brown. Place the baking dish on a baking sheet to catch any of the filling that may bubble over. Bake for 20 to 24 minutes or until the pastry turns golden brown. Serve immediately.

Empanadas are hand-held savory or sweet pastries. I have vivid memories of empanadas when traveling through Argentina where they are a daily staple. Serve with chimichurri, that most quintessential Argentinian piquant sauce. You can prepare it in a food processor, but I like to go "old school" and use a mortar and pestle. Uncooked empanadas freeze well. If you're short on time, you can find ready-made dough at specialty markets. This is my favorite Argentinian dish to make, and I have no doubt it will be yours too!

Mary's Empanadas

Makes approximately 30 to 36 empanadas

Prep Time: 40 minutes

Baking / Frying Time: 20 to 25 minutes

Dough

3 cups all-purpose flour

¼ teaspoon salt

¾ cup (6 ounces) unsalted butter, chilled and cut into ½-inch cubes

1 large egg

¼ to ½ cup water, as needed

Filling

3 tablespoons olive oil

2 medium onions, finely chopped

1 green bell pepper, seeds removed and finely chopped

2 pounds ground beef

2 tablespoons ground cumin

1 tablespoon smoked sweet paprika

2 teaspoons dried oregano

1 tablespoon chili powder

½ teaspoon garlic powder

½ teaspoon salt

¼ teaspoon ground black pepper

1 large tomato, seeded and chopped

3 hard-boiled eggs, peeled and sliced

½ cup pitted green olives (Picholine or Spanish preferred), cut in half lengthwise

2 large egg whites, for sealing the empanadas (save the egg yolk if baking the empanadas)

Chimichurri Sauce

1 large bunch parsley, coarsely chopped

1 large bunch cilantro, coarsely chopped

3 tablespoons capers, rinsed

2 garlic cloves, minced

1½ tablespoons red wine vinegar

1 teaspoon salt

¼ teaspoon red pepper flakes

¼ teaspoon ground black pepper

½ cup extra-virgin olive oil, as needed

1. To prepare the dough, place the flour and salt in the bowl of a food processor. Pulse to combine. With the processor on, slowly add the butter cubes through the feed tube. Add the egg and ¼ cup water. Continue to add water, pulsing the mixture as you go, until the dough forms a ball. Remove the dough from the processor and divide it into 2 balls. Using the palm of your hand, slightly flatten the balls into disks. Wrap in plastic wrap and refrigerate until ready to use.

2. Now it's time to make the filling. In a large sauté pan, over medium heat, heat the olive oil. Add the onions and sauté for 2 to 3 minutes. Add the bell pepper and sauté for 2 minutes more, or until the onions are translucent and the peppers are softened. Add the ground beef along with the cumin, paprika, oregano, chili powder, garlic powder, salt, and pepper. Cook the mixture on medium heat for approximately 5 minutes, using a wooden spoon to break up the meat. Add the tomatoes and cook for an additional 2 minutes to soften. Transfer the mixture to a mixing bowl and cool to room temperature. Once cool, cover with plastic wrap and refrigerate for 1 hour before making the empanadas.

3. When you are ready to assemble the empanadas, lightly flour your work surface. Remove 1 disk of dough from the refrigerator. Roll the dough out so that it is approximately ⅛-inch thick. Using a 4-inch round cutter, cut the dough into rounds. Place the dough rounds on a parchment-lined sheet pan. Place a generous amount of filling on one half of each round. You will want to keep a ½-inch edge free of filling. Top with a sliced egg and sliced olives. Continue with the remaining dough and filling.

4. In a small bowl, whisk the egg whites with a fork. If you are baking the empanadas, save the egg yolks for the glaze. Brush the edge of the empanada discs with the egg white mixture and fold over to create a half-moon shape. Twist and fold the empanada edge gently with your fingers or crimp the edge with a fork, making sure to get a good seal. Continue filling, folding, and crimping the remaining empanadas. Chill the filled empanadas in the refrigerator for at least 30 minutes before baking or frying them. While the empanadas are chilling, prepare the chimichurri sauce.

5. In a mixing bowl, combine the parsley, cilantro, capers, and garlic. Mix to combine. Add the vinegar, salt, red pepper flakes, and black pepper. Mix well. Drizzle in the olive oil to taste. The sauce is best if it is allowed to set at room temperature for 30 minutes *(continued)*

Mary's Empanadas

Continued

Baking Method

2 large egg yolks

2 tablespoons water

Frying Method

1 quart vegetable oil

6. The empanadas can be baked or fried. If baking, preheat the oven to 400 degrees. Place the chilled empanadas on a parchment-lined baking sheet. In a small bowl, combine the yolks and water. Using a pastry brush, brush the top of the empanadas with the egg wash. Bake for approximately 20 to 25 minutes or until golden brown. Serve with chimichurri sauce.

7. To fry the empanadas, heat 4 inches of oil in a large pot. Using a candy/oil thermometer, heat the oil to 365 degrees. Have a baking sheet lined with paper towels ready. Remove 2 to 3 empanadas at a time from the refrigerator. Carefully place in the hot oil and cook for a total of 5 minutes, turning the empanadas until both sides are golden brown. Remove from the oil and place on the paper towel-lined pan. Check the oil to make sure it is still at 365 degrees and continue with the remaining empanadas, 2 to 3 at a time. You may need to add additional oil as you fry them so that you keep the 4-inches of oil. Serve with chimichurri sauce.

Thinking "Outside the Tin"

You don't always need a traditional pie pan to make a fabulous pie. In this chapter, I share my favorite recipes made "outside the tin." Think hand pies, miniature tarts, cast iron pan pies, and my favorite, the Pavlova—a free-form meringue filled with oodles of whipped cream, lemon curd, and fresh fruit.

Hand pies are one of my favorite ways to enjoy a good pie. A hand pie has the filling of your choice wrapped in a pastry crust and perfectly sized to hold and eat with your hand. One of my favorites is a hand-held sour cherry pie made with Montmorency cherries. Who wouldn't want to have a cherry pie you can fit in your hand?

Miniature tarts come in all shapes and sizes. I give you two options. My lemon meringue pie bites are made in miniature muffin tins. Homemade lemon curd is topped with a brown sugar meringue creating the perfect mini pie. And who doesn't love a good s'more? My s'more tartlets bring that campfire feeling inside with a chocolate-ganache-filled graham cracker shell topped with homemade marshmallow. Get out the kitchen torch to finish 'em up!

If that's not enough to get you interested in this yummy chapter, there's also pastry-wrapped apples stuffed with brown sugar-spiced fruit and my chocolate chip salted caramel cookie pie made right in a cast iron skillet. It's fun to think outside the tin and live a little.

This tart is visually stunning, gluten-free, and vegan! Make my gluten-free pie pastry recipe using vegan butter for a vegan version. For a gluten-free only tart, you can use regular unsalted butter. Gluten-free flour is a challenge to work with. Don't be alarmed if the delicate dough tears or cracks when you place it in the tart pan. Just use your fingers to pinch it back together. The glossy pomegranate glaze makes the perfect resting place for a colorful medley of fruit. Apply your inner artist and design away with any fresh fruit you desire.

Gluten-Free Vegan Panna Cotta Tart with Pomegranate Glaze

Makes one 9-inch tart

Prep Time: 30 minutes
Baking Time: 18 to 21 minutes
Chilling Time: 2 hours

Crust

Gluten-Free Crust prepared with vegan butter alternative, page 35

plus a little additional gluten-free flour to dust your work surface

Filling

2 cups canned full-fat coconut milk, divided

2 teaspoons 100 percent agar powder

½ cup maple syrup

2 teaspoons vanilla extract

Glaze

1 cup pure pomegranate juice

1 teaspoon 100 percent agar powder

Garnish

Fresh berries

Fresh pomegranate arils

Fresh nectarines

Mint leaves

Edible flowers

1. Lightly spray a 9-inch round tart pan with a removable bottom with nonstick cooking spray. Place a round of parchment paper on pan bottom. Using gluten-free flour, lightly flour a piece of parchment paper. Place the pastry on the parchment paper and top with another piece of parchment paper. Roll the dough out into a 12-inch circle. Carefully remove the top piece of parchment and discard. Drape the dough gently in the pan. This is an extremely delicate dough as it is gluten-free. It may break but don't be alarmed! Just use your fingers to press the dough into the pan and pinch together any cracks that may occur. Use a rolling pin or sharp knife to trim the dough flush with the pan side. Refrigerate or freeze the dough-lined pan for 30 minutes.

2. Preheat the oven to 375 degrees. Remove the tart pan from the refrigerator or freezer and blind bake the crust. We will be baking the crust completely before filling the tart. Line the chilled tart crust with parchment paper. Fill with pie weights or dried beans. Make sure the weights are evenly distributed around the pan bottom. Bake until the edge of the crust starts to brown, about 12 to 13 minutes. Remove from the oven and carefully lift the parchment paper (with the weights) out of the tart pan. Using a fork, make 6 light pricks in the bottom of the crust, being careful not to go all the way through. Return pie crust to the oven and bake for 6 to 8 minutes or until the bottom of the crust is light brown. Remove from the oven and let cool on a rack for 15 minutes before filling the tart. For more information on blind baking a crust, see page 29.

3. For the filling, place 1 cup of coconut milk in a saucepan. Stir in the agar powder and mix to combine. Bring to a boil, whisking constantly. Reduce heat and cook on medium for 2 minutes, stirring frequently.

4. Remove from the heat. Whisk in the maple syrup, vanilla extract, and remaining 1 cup of coconut milk. Pour the mixture into the cooled tart shell and refrigerate until set, about 2 to 3 hours.

5. To prepare the glaze, pour the pomegranate juice into a saucepan. Add the remaining 1 teaspoon agar powder and mix to dissolve. Bring to a boil, whisking constantly. Reduce heat and cook on medium for 2 minutes, stirring frequently.

6. Allow the mixture to cool slightly. Carefully pour over the chilled panna cotta layer. Place back in the refrigerator for 2 hours to set.

7. When ready to serve, remove the tart pan side. Garnish with any or all of the garnish ideas provided.

Although I love baking pies all year long, there's something about fall that makes me want to bake them even more! I wait all year to gather my favorite apples at local farm markets and orchards. This apple dumpling recipe takes advantage of peak apple-picking season and marries a delicious filling of cinnamon, ginger, nuts, and berries. The result would be delectable as a baked apple, but the pastry takes it a step closer to a mini apple pie. I love to add a few pastry leaves on top of the pastry-wrapped apples to suggest an apple right off the tree.

Stuffed Apple in Pastry

Makes 6 stuffed apples

Prep Time: 1 hour
Baking Time: 40 minutes

Pastry
Mary's Favorite Pie Dough, page 30

Apples and Stuffing
6 large firm apples like Honeycrisp or Granny Smith
⅓ cup firmly packed brown sugar
½ teaspoon ground cinnamon
½ teaspoon ground ginger
6 tablespoons dried cranberries or dried cherries
2 tablespoons ground walnuts

Egg Wash
2 large eggs
3 tablespoons heavy cream

Garnish
Honey Caramel Sauce, page 223
Vanilla ice cream

1. Preheat the oven to 375 degrees. Line a baking sheet with parchment paper. Peel the apples. Using an apple corer and starting at the bottom of the apple, remove the core and seeds from the apple, keeping the top intact. Remove any stems that may still be on the apples.

2. In a mixing bowl, combine the brown sugar, ground cinnamon, ginger, dried fruit, and walnuts. Place the apples on a firm surface like a cutting board. Stuff the fruit mixture into the cored cavity. Try to make the filling as compact as possible.

3. In a bowl, combine the eggs with the cream. Set aside.

4. Divide the pastry dough into 8 pieces. You will use 6 pieces for the apples and the remaining 2 pieces to cut out pastry decorations. On a lightly floured work surface, roll 1 dough piece into a 7 by 7-inch square. Place an apple, stuffed side down, in the center of 1 dough piece. Brush the sides of dough with the egg wash mixture. Bring up dough sides and pinch firmly to adhere. Continue with remaining edges. Place on the prepared pan. Repeat the process with the remaining apples and dough pieces. Brush the entire exposed apple pastry with egg wash. Roll out the remaining dough pieces and cut out leaf decorations. Adhere the decorative leaves on the apple pastry using the egg wash. Brush top of the leaves with egg wash as well.

5. Bake the apples in the preheated oven until the pastry is nicely browned, about 40 minutes. Serve warm with ice cream and my honey caramel sauce.

I love chocolate chip cookie dough in all forms. I simply had to try it in a cast iron skillet because of the fun presentation. My family and friends tend to grab a spoon and start digging in. This pie also makes a great party food. I add pieces of caramel and Maldon sea salt because it just makes a good thing better, adding texture and that wonderful sweet-salty taste.

Cast Iron Chocolate Chip Cookie Pie with Sea Salt Caramel

Makes one 9-inch cast iron skillet pie

Prep Time: 35 minutes
Baking Time: 30 to 35 minutes

1 cup (8 ounces) plus 1 teaspoon softened unsalted butter, divided

1 cup granulated sugar

½ cup firmly packed light brown sugar

2 tablespoons pure maple syrup

1 teaspoon vanilla extract

2 large eggs

2½ cups flour plus 2 tablespoons, divided

1 teaspoon baking soda

½ teaspoon salt

¾ cup semi-sweet or bittersweet chocolate chunks (approximately ¼-inch square pieces)

¾ cup semi-sweet chocolate chips

½ cup caramel pieces

3 tablespoons heavy whipping cream

¾ teaspoon Maldon sea salt flakes, divided

1. Preheat the oven to 350 degrees. Lightly grease a 9-inch cast iron skillet with the 1 teaspoon of softened unsalted butter. Set aside.

2. In a stand mixer fitted with a paddle attachment, combine the remaining room temperature unsalted butter, white sugar, brown sugar, and maple syrup. Beat on medium speed to combine. Add the vanilla extract followed by the eggs, one at a time. This is a thick dough so I highly recommend using a stand mixer over a handheld mixer.

3. In a bowl, combine 2½ cups flour, baking soda, and regular salt. On medium-low speed, slowly add the flour mixture to the butter/egg mixture. With the mixer on low, add the chocolate chunks and chocolate chips.

4. In a small pan, place the caramel pieces and the heavy cream. Heat on low to slowly melt the caramel to make a smooth mixture. You can also melt the caramel pieces with the cream in a microwave, checking every 30 seconds and stirring until melted.

5. Dip your fingertips in the remaining 2 tablespoons of flour. Press half of the dough into the cast iron skillet using your floured fingertips. Drizzle the melted caramel on the dough. Sprinkle with ¼ teaspoon of the sea salt flakes.

6. Divide the remaining dough into thirds. Press each piece between your lightly floured hands to form 3 disks. Place the disks on top of the dough in the cast iron pan. Again using floured fingertips, press the dough disks to completely cover the bottom layer of dough and caramel sauce. Making the dough into flat disks makes it easier to place the remaining dough on top of the caramel.

7. Place the cast iron skillet on the center rack of the preheated oven. Bake for 30 to 35 minutes or until a toothpick comes out clean when placed in the center. Be careful not to over bake! The cookie pie will firm up as it cools.

8. Remove from the oven and let the cookie pie cool on a wire rack for 30 minutes. While cooling, sprinkle the top of the pie with the remaining ½ teaspoon sea salt flakes. Cut the cookie pie into wedges and serve with a scoop of vanilla ice cream.

Here's a fun way to enjoy a favorite camping treat indoors. Individual s'more tartlets feature a graham cracker crust, decadent bittersweet chocolate filling and a generous topping of homemade marshmallow, toasted to perfection with a kitchen torch. I like serving each guest their very own tartlet, but this recipe can also be prepared in an 8-inch tart pan.

S'more Tartlets with Homemade Marshmallows

Makes eight 4-inch tartlets or one 8-inch tart

Prep Time: 50 minutes
Baking Time: 6 to 10 minutes
Cooling Time: 6 hours

Crust

Mary's Favorite Graham Cracker Crust, page 34

Filling

12 ounces bittersweet chocolate, coarsely chopped

2 tablespoons unsalted butter, cut into pieces

1 cup heavy cream

Marshmallow Topping

2 envelopes unflavored gelatin (3 tablespoons plus 1½ teaspoons)

12 tablespoons water, divided

1½ cups granulated sugar

¾ cup light corn syrup

1. Preheat the oven to 350 degrees. Spray the bottom and side of eight 4-inch individual tart pans with nonstick cooking spray. Alternatively, you can make this recipe in an 8-inch tart pan. The full-size tart pan will also need to be sprayed with nonstick food spray and lined with a round of parchment paper. Line the tartlet or tart pan bottom and sides with the graham cracker crust. Make sure the mixture is pressed firmly so it is compact in the tart pans. If using tartlet pans, place them on a baking sheet. Chill the lined tart pans in the refrigerator or freezer for 30 minutes. Bake the smaller tart shells for 6 to 8 minutes and the larger tart shell for 10 minutes in the preheated oven. Remove and let cool completely on a cooling rack.

2. To prepare the filling, place the chopped chocolate and butter in a large bowl. In a saucepan, heat the cream over medium heat. Bring to a slow boil. Do not let it get to a full boil or it may boil over.

3. Slowly pour the hot cream over the chocolate mixture. Let sit for 1 minute then stir with a spatula until the chocolate and butter are completely melted and incorporated into the cream, making a smooth chocolate ganache.

4. Divide the ganache between the prepared tartlet pans or pour all the mixture into the large tart pan. Refrigerate for at least 6 hours or overnight to firm the ganache.

5. When ready to serve, prepare the marshmallow topping. Place the gelatin and 6 tablespoons of water in the bowl of a stand mixer fitted with the whip attachment. Let sit while you are preparing the sugar/corn syrup mixture.

6. Place the sugar, corn syrup, and remaining 6 tablespoons of water in a small heavy saucepan. Avoid using an aluminum pan as the sugar may crystallize on the pan side. *(continued)*

S'more Tartlets with Homemade Marshmallows

Continued

7. Heat on medium until the mixture reaches a temperature of 238 degrees. You will need a candy thermometer to check this. Once the temperature is reached, turn the mixer up to medium speed. Slowly and carefully pour the hot sugar syrup into the mixer. Once all the sugar water is added, increase the speed to medium high. Beat the mixture until it becomes white and fluffy, about 10 to 12 minutes.

8. You can either mound the marshmallow on top of each tart or place the marshmallow mixture into a disposable pastry bag fitted with a round tip. I prefer to unmold the tartlets or tart before topping with the marshmallow. It just makes serving a little easier. If you are mounding the mixture, make sure to spray your spatula or large spoon with nonstick cooking spray. The marshmallow mixture is very sticky, and this method will make it much easier to work with.

9. Once the marshmallow topping is on the tart or tartlets, get that handheld kitchen torch out and give the marshmallow a nice toasting. Individual tarts can be served as is. To cut a full-sized tart, get that nonstick cooking spray out again and spray your chef's knife on both sides. It will glide through that toasted marshmallow and make serving the larger tart a breeze!

Mary's tip: When piping the sticky marshmallow topping for a fancy swirl, use a disposable 18-inch pastry bag fitted with a round tip.

M

Most food historians trace the origins of the pavlova to a chef at an Australian hotel who created the dessert for famed visiting Russian ballerina Anna Pavlova. The billowy meringue was thought to represent the dancer's tutu! My stunning Pavlova is well worth the effort. The lemon curd can be prepared several days ahead and refrigerated but the meringue base needs to be prepared closer to the serving day.

Lemon Pavlova with Mascarpone Limoncello Crème

Makes 8 individual meringues

Prep Time: 1 hour
Baking Time: 1 hour
Rest Time: 2 hours

Pavlova Meringue
6 large egg whites, room temperature
¼ teaspoon cream of tartar
1½ cups extra fine sugar

Mascarpone Limoncello Crème
1¼ cup heavy cream, chilled
3 ounces mascarpone cheese, room temperature
¼ cup confectioners' sugar
1 tablespoon limoncello

Lemon Curd
A double recipe of my homemade lemon curd, page 216
or
2 cups purchased lemon curd

Fruit Garnish
Fresh berries like strawberries, blackberries, blueberries, raspberries, and red currants
Fresh mint sprigs

1. Prepare the oven and baking sheet. Preheat the oven to 200 degrees and adjust the rack to the lower part of the oven. Using a pencil, draw 8 circles on a piece of parchment paper. I use a glass to draw perfect circles. Turn the paper over so the outline faces the pan. Place the parchment on your baking sheet.

2. Prepare the meringue: Place the room temperature egg whites in the bowl of a stand mixer. Using the whip attachment, begin whipping the egg whites on medium speed. When egg whites become frothy, add the cream of tartar. Increase the speed to high. When whites begin forming medium peaks, start adding the sugar, about 2 tablespoons at a time. Continue to beat on high, adding the sugar as you go. When all the sugar has been added, whip whites for a few minutes until very stiff. The finished meringue should hold a very stiff peak.

3. Form the Pavlova base: Use a large spatula to mound the meringue around the outlined circles on your baking sheet. Using the back of the spatula, push the meringue from the center creating a divot like a volcano, with higher sides and a lower center.

4. Place the pan with the meringue on the lowest rack of your oven. Bake for 1 hour. Turn off the oven and crack open the oven door so it is slightly ajar. Let the meringue completely dry in the oven. If you have the time, let them sit in there for at least 2 hours. When the meringues are completely dry, use an offset spatula to loosen the meringue bottoms from the parchment paper. Carefully transfer the meringues to a serving platter. The meringues can be made several days ahead and stored at room temperature lightly covered with plastic wrap. Humidity does affect meringues so if it is hot and rainy, use the meringues right away or they will become soft.

5. When you are ready to serve the Pavlova, make the mascarpone limoncello crème. In a bowl of a stand mixer, place the heavy cream. Using the whip attachment, beat the cream until soft peaks form. With the mixer on medium, add the room temperature mascarpone, the confectioners' sugar, and the limoncello. Whip to just combine.

6. Fill the meringue with lemon curd. You may have more lemon curd than you need. Just store it in the fridge and enjoy a slathering on your morning toast or English muffin. Using a spatula, pile the mascarpone whipped cream on top of the lemon curd. Scatter the cleaned berries decoratively on top of the whipped cream and finish with a few decoratively placed mint sprigs.

I love high tea and my Lemon Blackberry Tartlets are always a big hit with family and friends alike. The rectangular shape of these tartlets makes for a simple yet lovely presentation. *Pâte sucrée* is my favorite pastry for dessert tarts and tartlets. Here, I nestle the lemon and blackberry filling into the sweet, tender French pastry. If you have never prepared high tea for your friends, I highly suggest it as a magical offering of love.

Lemon Blackberry Tartlets

Makes 8 tartlets

Prep Time: 40 minutes

Baking Time: 27 to 29 minutes

Crust

Pâte Sucrée (Sweet Pastry Crust),
page 32

Lemon Filling

4 large eggs

¾ cup superfine sugar

2 tablespoons finely grated lemon zest

¾ cup fresh lemon juice

½ cup heavy cream

Blackberry Sauce

4 cups fresh or frozen unsweetened
blackberries

¾ cup water

¾ cup granulated sugar

Garnish

A few fresh blackberries

Additional confectioners' sugar for dusting
the tartlets

Mint leaves

1. On a lightly floured work surface, roll the dough out into a ⅛-inch thickness. Cut the dough into 8 pieces slightly larger than the size of your tartlet pans. You can use 4-inch tartlet pans or small rectangular pans like I used in the photo. Spray the pans with nonstick cooking spray. Place the dough pieces into eight 4-inch individual tart tins. Using your fingers, press the dough onto the bottom and side of the pans. Using the tines of a fork, prick the bottoms of the pastry. Place the lined tart tins on a baking sheet and refrigerate or freeze for 30 minutes to chill.

2. Preheat the oven to 350 degrees. The tart shells will need to be blind baked. Remove the tart pans from the refrigerator or freezer. Line the pastry-lined tartlet pans with foil. Fill with pie weights or raw rice. Bake for 10 minutes. Carefully remove the foil and pie weights. Place the tartlet pans back in the oven and bake for an additional 5 minutes until lightly browned. Remove from the oven and let cool completely before filling.

3. Prepare the lemon filling. In a mixing bowl, combine the eggs, sugar, lemon zest, lemon juice, and cream. Using a wire whisk, beat until just combined. Pour the mixture through a strainer.

4. With the blind baked pastry shells still on the baking sheet, carefully pour the lemon mixture evenly into the tartlet shells. To make this easier, here's a tip. Transfer the lemon mixture into a glass measuring cup with a spout. Use the measuring cup to pour in the filling. Bake in the 350-degree oven until the middle of the tartlets are set, about 12 to 14 minutes. The center will be jiggly but firm to the touch. Remove from the oven and let cool completely before removing them from the tartlet pans.

5. Prepare the blackberry sauce. In a small saucepan, combine 4 cups of blackberries, ¾ cup water, and the sugar. Bring to a boil and simmer for 20 minutes or until the blackberries break down. Remove from the heat and strain through a fine-mesh sieve. Use the back of a spoon to gently push the mixture through. Cool the mixture and store in the refrigerator until ready to use.

6. When ready to serve, drizzle the top of the tartlets with chilled blackberry sauce. If you want, get creative and make a design like I did in the photo! Top with a few blackberries and mint leaves and give them a final dusting of confectioners' sugar. If there is any extra sauce, serve it on the side.

I loved Pop-Tarts™ as a child and cherry was my favorite flavor. These hand pies bring back happy memories of days gone by. If you make these in late July to mid-August, you may be lucky and find fresh tart Montmorency cherries at your local market. *Tip:* Keep the juice as you pit the cherries. You'll need it for the filling.

Tart Cherry Hand Pies

Makes twelve 3 by 5-inch rectangle hand pies

Prep Time: 40 minutes
Baking Time: 15 to 18 minutes

Crust
Mary's Favorite Pie Dough, page 30

Filling
4 cups (about 1 pound) fresh
Montmorency cherries or thawed frozen
Montmorency cherries
⅔ cup granulated sugar
2 tablespoons cornstarch
½ teaspoon fresh lemon juice
1 teaspoon almond extract

Egg Wash and Topping
1 large egg
1 tablespoon heavy cream

Optional Fillings
¼ cup chopped walnuts
¼ cup chopped bittersweet or semi-sweet
chocolate

Optional Topping
Confectioners' sugar glaze (1½ cups
sifted confectioners' sugar mixed with
1 to 2 tablespoons water)

1. Preheat the oven to 350 degrees. Prepare the filling. In a mixing bowl, combine the cherries and sugar. Let rest for 10 minutes. Place a colander over another mixing bowl. Place the cherries in the colander, catching the excess cherry juice in the bowl. Place the drained cherries in a mixing bowl and set aside. Keep any strained cherry juice.

2. Place the strained cherry juice, cornstarch, and lemon juice in a small pot. Stirring continuously over low heat, cook the mixture for approximately 5 minutes or until it bubbles and becomes thick. Remove from the heat and stir in the almond extract. Let the mixture cool for 5 minutes.

3. Using a rubber spatula, transfer the thickened cherry juice mixture to the bowl of reserved cherries. Carefully toss the cherries with the thickened juice to coat. If using the walnuts and chocolate chips, fold them into the mixture now.

4. Line a baking sheet with parchment paper. On a lightly floured work surface, roll out 1 dough disk into a ⅛-inch thickness and cut into twelve 5 by 3-inch rectangles. Place pastry rectangles on the prepared pan. In a small bowl, combine the large egg and 1 tablespoon heavy cream to make an egg wash. Lightly brush the pastry sides with the egg wash. Place a scant ¼ cup of the filling in the center of the pastry rectangles.

5. Roll out the remaining dough disk and cut 12 more rectangles. Place the pastry rectangles on top of the pastry that have cherry filling. Using the tines of a fork, go around the pastry edge and press to adhere.

6. Brush the top of the hand pies with egg wash. Use a toothpick or paring knife to make steam holes or vents in the top of each hand pie.

7. Bake in the preheated oven until nicely browned, approximately 15 to 18 minutes. Remove pie from the baking sheet and let cool on a wire rack.

8. If desired, drizzle with confectioners' sugar glaze.

On my inaugural trip to Paris, tarte Tatin was the first dessert I tried. I loved it so much, I think I ordered it at every meal. You can easily swap out the traditional apple version for pear, but I hold the pear version close to my heart. What makes my recipe special is the addition of a rich caramel made from my spiced red wine reduction.

Pinot Noir Pear Tarte Tatin

Makes one 9-inch pear tarte Tatin

Prep Time: 1 hour
Baking Time: 25 minutes

5 Bartlett pears, peeled and cored
2 tablespoons fresh lemon juice
1¼ cups sugar, divided
1 sheet frozen puff pastry, thawed
¾ cup Pinot Noir
1 cinnamon stick
2 whole star anise
6 tablespoons (3 ounces) unsalted butter,
cut into ½-inch cubes

1. Place the peeled and cored pears, cored side down, on a cutting board and cut into quarters. Place the quartered pears in a mixing bowl and toss with the lemon juice and ¼ cup sugar. Let sit for 30 minutes.

2. Lightly flour a work surface and roll out the puff pastry. Cut out a 10-inch round of pastry. I like to set the cast iron skillet upside down on the pastry then cut about ½-inch more around the pan to create my round. Place the pastry round on a piece of parchment paper and refrigerate while preparing the tart filling.

3. Preheat the oven to 425 degrees. Place the wine, cinnamon stick, and star anise in a small sauce pot. Heat on medium and simmer until reduced to about 2 tablespoons. Remove and discard the cinnamon stick and star anise.

4. While the red wine is reducing, prepare the sugar and butter mixture. In a cast iron skillet, melt the butter on medium-low heat. When melted, add the remaining 1 cup sugar. Increase heat to medium and cook the sugar, stirring now and then, until it becomes a light caramel color. Add the red wine reduction and stir until combined. Turn off the heat.

5. Drain the pears in a colander. Discard the liquid. Using metal tongs, carefully arrange the pears in the cast iron skillet with the slim side facing the center. The pears should fit snugly. Place the puff pastry round on top of the pears and cut 4 small slits on top to allow steam to be released during the baking process.

6. Place the pan on a baking sheet. Place on the middle rack of the preheated oven. Bake for 25 minutes. The top pastry should be nicely browned.

7. Very carefully remove the baking sheet from the oven. The cast iron skillet will be extremely hot so make sure you have your heavy-duty kitchen mitts on! Using a turkey baster, extract the extra liquid from the cast iron skillet and transfer it to a small saucepan.

8. Place a piece of parchment paper on your work surface. Now place your serving platter on top of the cast iron skillet and very carefully flip the pan and plate over. The Tatin should easily release onto your serving platter. The parchment paper will catch any excess liquid that comes out of the pan and makes clean up much easier.

9. Heat the reserved juices on medium-low heat until thickened. The juice should be the consistency of a glaze. Remove from the heat and brush the pear slices with the thickened juice. Your pear tarte Tatin is ready to serve!

My friend Steve absolutely loves lemon meringue pie. Whenever he comes to town, I make a special effort to share my Lemon Meringue Pie Bites. He loves that I make lemon curd from scratch. Steve says you can really taste the difference, and I agree! He and other fans of this recipe appreciate the tiny size of the bites so they can sneak and eat as many as they want. And, you will absolutely love my Italian brown sugar meringue. It's a luscious and very stable meringue so you can decorate ahead of time.

Lemon Meringue Pie Bites

Makes 2 dozen

Prep Time: 1 hour
Baking Time: 13 to 15 minutes

Crust
Pâte Sucrée, page 32

Filling
A double recipe of my homemade
lemon curd, page 216
or
2 (10 ounce) jars of purchased lemon curd

Meringue Topping
½ cup (4 large) egg whites,
room temperature
1 cup firmly packed brown sugar
¼ cup water
⅛ teaspoon cream of tartar

1. You will need two 12-well miniature muffin tins for this recipe. Spray the inside of each well with nonstick cooking spray.

2. Lightly dust your work surface with flour and roll a dough disk into a 12-inch round. Cut the dough into rounds using a 2½-inch round cookie cutter. Using your fingers, gently press the dough rounds into the pan, making sure the dough side goes all the way up the muffin wells. Also make sure the dough is firmly on the bottom of each cup. You want the miniature shells to come out with a flat bottom. I like to use a pastry dough tamper to make this job easier. Continue with the remaining dough as needed to line all 24 muffin wells. You may not need all the dough. Simply roll the leftover dough into a ball and push down with the palm of your hand to make a disk. Cover with plastic wrap and refrigerate or freeze the dough for another use.

3. Place the lined muffin tins in the freezer for 30 minutes. This will prevent the dough from shrinking as the miniature pie shells are baked. About 15 minutes before removing the tins from the freezer, preheat your oven to 350 degrees.

4. Bake in the preheated oven until the miniature crusts are a light golden color, about 13 to 15 minutes. Check the shells halfway through the baking process. If you see them shrinking on the side, just take the back of a teaspoon and gently push the dough back up. Remove the pan from the oven and let the shells cool in the pan.

5. When cool, use a spoon to gently lift the pastry shells out of the tin. Place the baked shells on a baking sheet. Fill each pastry shell with lemon curd. Place in the refrigerator while preparing the meringue. Remember that any leftover lemon curd can be stored in the refrigerator and used on English muffins, toast, or my favorite, a croissant!

6. Place the egg whites into the bowl of a stand mixer fitted with a whip attachment. Place the brown sugar and water in a small saucepan over medium heat. Heat the mixture on high to the soft-ball stage (245 degrees). Use a candy thermometer to check the temperature. Do not stir the mixture, however you can "swirl" the pan now and then to remove any excess sugar buildup that may form on the pan side. *(continued)*

Lemon Meringue Pie Bites

Continued

7. While the sugar mixture is cooking, start whipping the egg whites on medium speed. When the whites are foamy, add the cream of tartar. Increase speed to high and beat until egg whites are fairly stiff. Reduce the speed to medium and slowly pour the hot sugar mixture into the whites. When all the sugar is added, increase speed to medium high. Beat 5 to 6 minutes. The mixture should be very stiff but still slightly warm. You can tell when the meringue is done by placing your hands on the bottom of the bowl. If it is no longer hot, the meringue is cool enough to use.

8. Using a teaspoon or a pastry bag fitted with a star or round tip, top each miniature pie with a generous dollop of meringue. Using a kitchen torch, brown the meringue topping. The miniature pie bites can be frozen at this stage. Just remove about 15 minutes before serving and give the meringue a "touch up" with your kitchen torch!

Finishing Touches

In this chapter, I share my favorite recipes that will put your
pies over the top! I'm talking chocolate curls, homemade
dulce de leche, tart lemon curd, fudgy chocolate sauce, and
candied citrus peel.

But don't think these recipes are only for pies. These versatile
recipes have many other delicious uses. Spread that lemon
curd on your morning toast or scone. My homemade dulce
de leche is perfect with a warm croissant or smeared on top
of a banana. Homemade bittersweet chocolate sauce
is perfect over ice cream. And that honey caramel sauce?
Don't get me started. It's truly the bee's knees!

When making lemon curd, I prefer using Meyer lemons, which taste like a cross between a traditional lemon and a mandarin orange. The fruit is very tender and extremely juicy with a peel that is thinner than a regular lemon. If Meyer lemons are not available, substitute Lisbon, Eureka, or Bearss lemons for the recipe.

Lemon Curd

Makes approximately 1¼ cups lemon curd

½ cup granulated sugar, divided

Zest of 2 lemons

4 large egg yolks

¼ cup freshly squeezed lemon juice
(preferably from Meyer lemons)

3 tablespoons unsalted butter,
cut into pieces

1. In a medium mixing bowl, whisk together ¼ cup of the sugar, zest, and egg yolks. Set aside.

2. In a medium saucepan, bring the lemon juice and remaining ¼ cup sugar to a boil over medium heat. Gradually whisk in half of the hot mixture into the yolk mixture. Add the egg yolk mixture to the remaining hot lemon mixture in the pot. Cook on low heat, stirring constantly, until thickened, about 3 to 4 minutes. Be careful not to overheat or the eggs will curdle on the bottom of the pan. If this happens, simply pass the curd through a sieve to remove any cooked egg pieces.

3. Transfer the curd to a clean bowl. Gradually whisk in the butter until incorporated. Place a piece of plastic wrap on top of the curd, pressing down so the film touches the curd. This will avoid the curd from forming a crust. When cool, place in the refrigerator until ready to use. The curd will last for up to 1 week.

Candied citrus from scratch takes some time, but it is *so* worth the effort. Your candied citrus will last several months in a food safe bag in the freezer.

Candied Citrus

4 lemons or 3 navel oranges (preferably organic) washed

1 cup water, plus more for blanching

1 cup granulated sugar

¾ cup extra-fine sugar for coating the citrus to finish

1. Slice off the ends of the citrus. Using a sharp paring knife, peel off the skin and remove as much of the white pith as possible. Now, use a chef's knife to thinly slice the peels. You can use the peeled citrus for eating or juicing. For candied citrus slices, cut very thin round slices of skin-on citrus and remove any seeds.

2. Bring a large pot of water to a boil. Add the citrus peels or slices and cook for 15 minutes. Drain in a colander and rinse. Pat them dry with a paper towel, then rinse again under cold water. The blanching and rinsing removes the bitter flavor of the remaining pith and softens the citrus peels or slices.

3. In a large pot, combine 1 cup water with 1 cup sugar. Heat on medium, stirring often, until the sugar is dissolved. Bring to a low boil then add all the blanched citrus peel or slices. Reduce heat and simmer for 45 minutes.

4. Place the extra-fine sugar in a plastic food storage bag. Drain the citrus in a colander, catching the syrup in a bowl placed underneath. *Tip:* Let the sugar mixture cool and store in the refrigerator for later use as a sweetener for iced tea, a delicious and refreshing combination.

5. Place the peel or slices in the plastic bag with the extra fine sugar and gently shake to coat the citrus. Spread the candied citrus on a wire rack to cool and dry completely. I like to place a piece of wax paper or parchment underneath the rack to catch any excess sugar. It will take 1 to 2 days for the citrus to completely dry. Store in an airtight container in a cool, dry place and store for up to a month. You can also freeze the citrus and use as needed.

I love anything chai! Making your own chai spice mix makes it easy to add this warm and comforting spice blend to everything from scone batter and pies to smoothies and lattes.

You can easily make your own mix by using ground spices but if you want to really get that something extra, try making it with whole spices. Either is delicious. Believe me, you'll be happy to have this versatile spice blend on hand in your pantry.

Mary's Homemade Chai Spice Mix
Ground Chai Spice Mixture

2 teaspoons ground cinnamon

2 teaspoons ground ginger

2 teaspoons cardamom

1 teaspoon ground cloves

1 teaspoon ground coriander

1. In a bowl, combine all of the spices. Mix to combine. Store in the pantry until ready to use.

Mary's Homemade Chai Spice Mix
Whole Chai Spice Mixture

1 tablespoon green whole cardamom

3 whole star anise pods

1 teaspoon coriander seeds

½ teaspoon ground ginger

1 cinnamon stick, broken in pieces

½ teaspoon ground nutmeg

4 whole cloves

7 allspice berries

½ teaspoon white peppercorns

1. Using a chef's knife, coarsely chop the cardamom and star anise pods. You only need to do a coarse chop to get the process going. Place in a mixing bowl.

2. Add all the remaining ingredients into the bowl with the cardamom and star anise and mix to combine.

3. Working in batches, place the mixture in either a spice grinder or process by hand using a mortar and pestle. Store the ground spices in the pantry until ready to use.

In Latin American countries dulce de leche, or sweet caramelized milk, is a popular ingredient used in desserts and cookies. The recipes below use either whole milk (for the longer version done on the stovetop) or sweetened condensed milk (the shorter version which is done in the oven). A version made with goat milk is called cajeta and is popular in Mexico.

Dulce de Leche
Oven Version

1 can (14 ounces) sweetened condensed milk

A few flecks of coarse sea salt

1. Preheat the oven to 425 degrees. Pour 1 can of sweetened condensed milk into a glass pie pan or shallow baking dish. Stir in a few flecks of sea salt.

2. Cover the pie plate snugly with aluminum foil. Set the pie plate within a larger pan that has 2-inch sides. Add hot water until it reaches halfway up the side of the pie pan. Bake for 1¼ to 1½ hours. Carefully check mixture during baking, adding more water as needed to the larger pan.

3. Remove the foil. The dulce de leche should be a medium caramel color. Remove from the oven and cool. The mixture will thicken as it cools. Once cool, use a wire whisk to smooth out the mixture. Store in the refrigerator for up to 2 weeks.

Dulce de Leche
Stovetop Version

4 cups whole milk or goat milk

4 cups granulated sugar

1 tablespoon vanilla extract

2 tablespoons corn syrup

1. In a heavy medium pot, combine the milk, sugar, vanilla, and corn syrup. Bring mixture to a gentle simmer and cook over very low heat, stirring frequently, until slightly thickened and golden brown; about 2½ to 3 hours.

2. The mixture will thicken as it cools. Use a wire whisk to smooth out the mixture. Store in the refrigerator for up to 2 weeks.

Chocolate curls are like snowflakes. No two are alike yet all are beautiful. They are easy to make and hey, if you don't like how one turns out you can remelt the chocolate! Use the best chocolate you can find. I avoid using chocolate chips that have additives. Just check the ingredient list before you buy your chocolate. Make sure you just see one ingredient: chocolate! My two favorite brands of chocolate are Callebaut™ and Valrhona™.

Chocolate Curls

4 ounces bittersweet chocolate

2 teaspoons unsalted butter, cut into pieces

1. Place the chocolate and butter in a microwavable bowl. Melt the chocolate in the microwave using 20-second bursts until completely melted. Use a heat-resistant spatula to stir the chocolate in between bursts of heat.

2. Pour the chocolate on the back of a baking sheet. Using an offset spatula, spread the chocolate out as thinly as possible. Place in the freezer for 3 to 4 minutes or until just firm. Using a dough scraper, scrape the chocolate in large strokes to make curls. If the chocolate gets too soft, just place it in the freezer for a minute.

3. Store the chocolate curls in the freezer in a container with parchment or wax paper between layers of the curls. When ready to use, remove from the freezer and decorate your dessert.

If you are going to splurge on one ingredient, make it chocolate! Go for a top-quality European chocolate like Callebaut™ or Valrhona™. And go for bittersweet chocolate that contains a minimum of 70 percent cacao and has less sugar than a semisweet chocolate. Although you can use the two chocolates interchangeably when baking, bittersweet chocolate will give you a deeper, more intense flavor.

Bittersweet Chocolate Sauce

Makes approximately 2 cups

½ cup brown sugar

¾ cup heavy cream

5 ounces bittersweet chocolate, coarsely chopped

2 tablespoons unsalted butter, cut into chunks

2 tablespoons orange-flavored or coffee-flavored liqueur, optional

1. Place the sugar, cream, chocolate, and butter in a heat-proof bowl. Place the bowl over a pot of simmering water. The water should not touch the bottom of the bowl. Simmer for about 12 minutes without stirring. The chocolate should almost be completely melted before you start stirring.

2. Take the bowl off of the water (use pot holders!) and whisk in the liqueur if using. The sauce can be used warm or may be cooled then stored in the refrigerator for up to 1 week. The sauce will thicken in the fridge, so I like to store it in a heat-proof jar so I can warm it up in a microwave. A few spurts of microwave heat, and your sauce will be ready to go!

The main difference between chocolate sauce and fudge sauce is the texture. Hot fudge sauce is thicker and richer while chocolate sauce is thinner and more pourable. Chocolate sauce stays liquid in the refrigerator, while hot fudge sauce gets cold and thick…like fudge. But it's simple to get back to a delicious, pourable consistency by heating it in the microwave.

Mary's Easy Hot Fudge Sauce

1 can (14 ounces) sweetened condensed milk

1 cup bittersweet chocolate, coarsely chopped

2 tablespoons unsalted butter

1 tablespoon of your favorite liqueur like Kahlua, Bailey's Irish Cream™, or Amaretto™, optional

1. In a small pot, combine the sweetened condensed milk and chocolate. Heat on medium heat, stirring constantly, until chocolate is melted.

2. Remove from the heat and stir in the butter until melted. If using liqueur, add and stir to combine.

3. Let the sauce cool very slightly to thicken and serve immediately or store in a jar or microwavable container in the refrigerator for up to 5 days. To reheat, place the jar or container in the microwave and heat in 30-second increments, stirring between each spurt, until melted and smooth.

This is my "go to" caramel sauce. No sugar boiling involved; just combine all the ingredients, simmer, and enjoy! Because of all the local honey available to me at our farm (and because my husband Billy just loves honey) I always have some of this delicious sauce on hand.

Honey Caramel Sauce

Makes approximately 1 cup

½ cup firmly packed dark or light brown sugar

3 tablespoons unsalted butter, cut into cubes

½ cup honey

¼ teaspoon salt

¼ cup heavy cream

1 to 2 teaspoons honey-flavored liqueur such as Koval Honey™ liqueur, optional

1. In a heavy-bottomed medium-sized pot, combine the sugar, butter, honey, and salt. Place on low heat. Stir the mixture constantly until the butter is melted and the mixture is evenly combined.

2. Add the cream and liqueur if using. Bring back to a simmer, stirring to combine. Remove from the heat and let the mixture cool slightly. The sauce will thicken as it cools. Serve immediately or transfer to a glass jar and store in the refrigerator for up to 5 days. If the sauce becomes too thick after being refrigerated, simply reheat in the microwave.

Crème fraîche is a thickened soured cream. Although you can find it at specialty markets, it's easy to make at home. You just need to remember to make it ahead–the mixture needs to sit at room temperature for 12 hours.

Homemade Crème Frâiche

2 cups heavy cream

2 tablespoons buttermilk

Combine the cream and buttermilk in a non-reactive (not metal) container. I use a glass bowl. Cover with plastic wrap and allow to sit at room temperature for 12 hours. The mixture will thicken as it sits. Store in the refrigerator in a covered container for up to 2 weeks.

Index

Acknowledgments

This pie book came together through the efforts of numerous talented people who did not hold back on their loving care of me and my recipes. All of them gave their very best to make this book a reality.

To Terri Milligan, my recipe editor, who's talent and dedication never ceases to amaze me. I appreciate all that you do and count you as a dear friend.

To Anne-Marie St. Germaine, my writer. Thank you for stepping in when we needed you most and bringing my stories to life.

To Bill Strong, my writer. Thank you for your brilliant writing and your wonderful sense of humor.

To Deirdre Boland, art direction and design. Your talent, vision, and energy is something to behold. Simply put, you are creative magic.

To Brett Hawthorne, my graphic designer. Thank you for your attention to detail. I always felt like I was in good hands.

To Johanna Brannan Lowe, my food and prop stylist. You are truly brilliant. You took each of my pie recipes and turned them into unbelievable shots with those angel hands.

To Paul Strabbing, my photographer. You captured the beauty and essence of each pie perfectly. Did I mention you are also a pure joy to work with?

And most importantly to my husband William. Thank you for believing in me, encouraging me, and unconditionally loving me. You are my best pie taster and the true love of my life.

Mary DiSomma

My Life in Pies is just one facet of the elegant and approachable world of Mary DiSomma.

Mary, an enthusiastic and imaginative baker, is the author of *A Gift of Cookies: Recipes to Share with Family & Friends*. As she explains, "Cookies are a quintessential part of my story. I've been baking them since I was a little girl. In fact, my Italian-American grandmother, mother, and aunts taught me everything I know. They were my 'cooking school.' In the kitchens of the women in my family, I inherited the tips and tricks of the generations."

Mary's loves to share her recipes and tips with others. She is a celebrated food blogger and has a YouTube Cooking Show focusing on her delicious recipes and cooking techniques.

All this, and she still continues to bake over 7,000 cookies every year just to give away to family and friends during the holidays.

Mary DiSomma's Signature Kitchen Collection

To Mary, the tools of the trade are just as important as the recipes. Mary DiSomma's Signature Kitchen Collection features timeless and exquisitely designed kitchen tools, textiles, and specialty baking items including Mary's Cognac Barrel-Aged Vanilla which she uses in all her baking.

"I want to be surrounded by tools that look beautiful and feel good in my hands. My signature floral print design that was inspired by a trip to New York is found throughout my collection. The ceramics are a nod to my love of ceramic kitchenware from Ireland and an example of my approach to home decor: using multiple textures, patterns, and colors for rich, multi-layered, and unique designs."

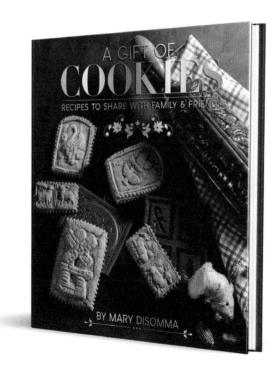

Visit Mary's blog and marketplace at MARYDISOMMA.COM

233